HERE'S LOOKING AT YOU, KID!

Ireland Goes to the Pictures

Stephanie McBride teaches film and media studies at Dublin City University. Former Chair of the Junior Dublin Film Festival, she is a member of the Board of the Film Institute of Ireland.

Roddy Flynn teaches at the School of Communications, in Dublin City University. He works as a researcher on the Irish film industry and writes for *Film Ireland*.

HERE'S LOOKING AT YOU, KID!

Ireland Goes to the Pictures

Edited by
Stephanie McBride & Roddy Flynn

WOLFHOUND PRESS

First published in 1996 by
Wolfhound Press, Ltd
68 Mountjoy Square
Dublin 1, Ireland.

Editorial © 1996 Stephanie McBride and Roddy Flynn
Text and illustrations © as credited in acknowledgements

Wolfhound Press receives financial assistance from the Arts Council/
An Chomhairle Ealaíon, Dublin.

British Library Cataloguing in Publication Data
A catalogue record for this book is available from the British Library

ISBN 0-86327-556-7

Cover photograph: G.A. Duncan: 'The Palace of Dreams', the Savoy, 1955
Cover design: Slick Fish Design, Dublin
Typesetting: Wolfhound Press
Printed and bound in Great Britain by Hartnolls Ltd, Bodmin, Cornwall

CONTENTS

FOREWORD

The Junior Dublin Film Festival is very proud to present *Here's Looking at You, Kid: Ireland Goes to the Pictures* as part of its contribution to the centenary of cinema. The Festival is dedicated to bringing the world of cinema, in all its diversity, to children and young people. Our aim is to enhance the enjoyment and understanding of film, through a range of activities. In this context, we felt it was appropriate to explore early memories of film in Ireland over the years.

It is clear from the contributions to this book that early experiences of cinema are both similar and diverse, fearful and fascinating. The phrase 'windows of wonder' comes to mind. Our initial contact with film and its social space provides us with potent glimpses of the wider world as we continue a journey to (re)discover who we are.

Stephanie McBride, a founding member of the Junior Dublin Film Festival, and Roddy Flynn have produced a book which is itself a window of wonder, providing us with an opportunity to enjoy and reflect upon a variety of individual responses to this most powerful of story-telling forms.

The Festival is indebted to them and deeply appreciative of the enthusiasm, expertise and commitment with which they have tackled this endeavour. On behalf of the Board of Directors, I would like to express sincere gratitude to those without whom there would be no book – the contributors – for their generosity of spirit in giving their time and energy to this project.

Enjoy!

Padraic Mulholland
Chairman,
Junior Dublin Film Festival

ACKNOWLEDGEMENTS

Special thanks to:
- Michael Cunningham, who first suggested the idea
- my parents, Neil and Mary McBride, who introduced me to 'the palace of delights' – the Erne cinema, Ballyshannon, and later the Abbey cinema
- and my parents, Richard and Mary Flynn, for constantly encouraging my obsession with cinema (keep taping those videos!)
- Alison Finch for her enthusiastic work in the early stages of the project
- Alan Robinson for his enthusiastic work during the later stages of the project
- members of the Board of the Junior Dublin Film Festival
- Niamh O'Sullivan, Chair, Film Institute of Ireland
- Kevin Rockett, Red Mountain Press
- Peter Sirr, Director, Irish Writers' Centre, for his help and facilities
- Tanya Kiang and Gemma Tipton, CIRCA Art Magazine
- Sunniva O' Flynn, Liam Wylie and Suzanne Campbell, Archive, Film Institute of Ireland
- Sarah McCarthy, Film Institute of Ireland
- Grace Duncan
- Donal Haughey, Celine Curtin, Patsy Murphy and Clare Scally, Galway Film Resource Centre
- Nicki Carter
- Susan, Ciara, Eilís and all at Wolfhound Press

Photo Credits
Section 1
Pages 1, 3, 6, G.A. Duncan
page 2, reproduced by kind permission of Kevin Rockett, Red Mountain Press
page 5, From *The Genius of Father Browne* by E.E. O'Donnell, Wolfhound Press, 1990 . Print courtesy of David Davison.
page 7, (top) reproduced by kind permission of the Ulster Museum, print courtesy of the Film Institute of Ireland; (bottom) print courtesy of David Bigger
page 8, (top) print courtesy of Donal Haughey; (bottom) reproduced by kind permission of Jim Garry, from the journal of the Old Drogeda Society, 1990, no. 7. Print courtesy of Film Institute of Ireland

Section 2
Page 1, reproduced by kind permission of Kevin Rockett, Red Mountain Press
page 2, (top) courtesy of Film Institute of Ireland; (bottom) G.A. Duncan
page 3, (top) print courtesy of British Film Institute; (bottom) G.A. Duncan
page 4, (top) print courtesy of Film Institute of Ireland; (bottom) print courtesy of Joan Kiernan
page 5, G.A. Duncan
page 6, (top) print courtesy of Tipperary Excel Heritage; (bottom) courtesy of Film Institute of Ireland
page 7, prints courtesy of the British Film Institute
page 8, G.A. Duncan

Extracts
Extract from *Sam's Fall* by Richard Kearney, by kind permission, Sceptre
Extract from *The Woman's Daughter* by Dermot Bolger, published by Penguin Books, reproduced by kind permission of Dermot Bolger & A. P. Watt Ltd, London.
St Mary's Hall by Frank McGuinness, by kind permission, Gallery Press
Contribution by Mary Cummins first published in the *Irish Times*, 28 March 1996

PROLOGUE

Christmas 1976, and the P.E. Hall at St Oliver Plunkett's National School, Malahide, becomes my first cinema. All expense has been spared to create that cinema ambience: instead of subtle recessed lighting fading to black velvet as the picture rolls, every corner of the hall is illuminated by stark fluorescent lighting; when it is switched off, the hall is reduced to a dusk-like gloom by the black plastic bags taped over the windows. Furthermore, like the Wizard of Oz, the mechanics of the magic to follow are exposed for all to see: at the back of the hall a teacher fiddles with a 16mm projector sitting on a gym horse. All the painstaking technique, learnt the previous Christmas, of threading film through the maze of projector spools has been lost. As the knowledge is re-acquired through trial and error (although it will be forgotten again by next year's party), four hundred children are herded into their allotted seats. Despite constant imprecations from pleading teachers to 'shush!', the air is rent with shouts and screams. The teachers' efforts are rendered fruitless by their lack of co-ordination – one class at a time, perhaps thirty kids, quietens, then starts up again as it becomes obvious that the other three hundred and fifty are still shrieking. Relative silence only comes when the cartoons – now memorable only as vivid flashes of bright colour – start rolling. Half an hour later, the lights blink on again for a brief intermission and we queue for refreshments: popcorn, a small packet of sweets (Trebor's Refreshers) and the kind of cheap diluted orange juice that leaves you gagging for five minutes after you crush your thin plastic cup.

As the coughs from the orange-drinkers subside, the fluorescent lights vanish a second time, prompting another burst of 'Woooo's from the sixth classes. However, as the main feature – a six-year-old print of Scrooge, the 1970 version of Dickens's A Christmas Carol, with Albert Finney in the title role – starts, real silence reigns for the first time. After nearly twenty years, memory of the film is hazy: nothing of the plot (or of the cast, except Finney) remains, beyond one startling sequence. To finally convince Scrooge of the dire consequences of pursuing his miserly existence, the Ghost of Christmas to Come brings him on a bleak tour of his own future which concludes at his own gravestone. Scrooge falls to his knees, sobbing in terror as he reads his own epitaph: the ground suddenly crumbles beneath him and he falls headlong through darkness into a world of phantoms, lost souls drifting through purgatory. These drift past the terrified

Scrooge, until his attention (and that of the audience, now watching from his point of view) is unavoidably drawn to a single distant but rapidly-approaching spectre. All eyes focus on this single demon, as its skeletal visage comes to fill the screen. It pauses briefly, floating before the camera, then with a ghastly smile opens its mouth and surges forward – through the screen. There is instant bedlam in the hall. A wave of fear ripples through the assembled throng, striking and then passing me, only mildly dissipating as it reaches the older kids nearer the back. Several junior infants are led or carried away, initial shock quickly transmogrifying into tears. And the film plays on.

* * *

Some twenty years on, putting this book together, I considered my own memories of the cinema and recalled *Scrooge*. Having only the fragments above to go on, I looked it up in a Film Guide for more detailed information. All seemed well: the film did exist, and a glance at the cast list prompted a few buried memories. But then I noticed a reference to the film's 'anaemic and piffling' songs. Confused, I looked for the genre classification: 'musical adaptation'. How can this be? *Scrooge* was the standard by which I judged subsequent horror films. I remembered (and still remember) no songs. But there it is in black and white: my horror picture was everyone else's musical.

It might be argued that seven hundred people sitting in a cinema see seven hundred different films, filtering what they see through their personal subjectivities and idiosyncrasies. If this is the case, it is doubly true for children – and it is this that *Here's Looking at You, Kid* celebrates. Bring a child to the cinema for the first time and all the rules he or she has learnt about how the world works are stood on their heads: faces are twenty feet tall and fill the screen; years pass in a second; and worlds that could only previously have been conceived of in a dream or nightmare suddenly appear, apparently real, with an implicit existence beyond the edge of the cinema-screen. The order of the world outside the cinema is gone, and suddenly anything is possible. Even afterwards, memories of what filled their fields of vision and hearing for the previous two hours continue to reverberate through their heads. Reality and imagination meet to form something infinitely richer than either could have created alone.

Cinema's place in our lives may change as we grow older. The innocence we bring to the cinema as children is often lost to us as adults, although other cinematic pleasures emerge (particularly as romance slips off the screen and into the stalls). But the beautiful paradox that cinema permits can never be totally eclipsed: how can the facility to walk off the reality of a damp, cold street, through a lobby, and into a finite room containing infinite possibility be anything other than magic?

ROMANCE
OR
ALL THAT HEAVEN ALLOWS

Joseph O'Connor

The first film I ever saw in a cinema was *War and Peace*, starring Henry Fonda and Audrey Hepburn. The cinema was on the main street in Dun Laoghaire – it isn't there any more, and I have to confess with some shame and frustration that I can't remember its name, despite much brain-racking and carpet-pacing. Anyway, it was fantastically exciting to be going to the pictures at all, and I was knocked out by the storming sound and fabulous fury of the movie with its epic battle scenes and colourful costumes and generally swashbuckling style. But even more gripping than the film itself was the fact that it was so long it had to be shown in two parts: Part One was running for one week and Part Two could be seen the week after that! For a child reared on the ten-minute-instant-hit culture of children's TV, this was an astonishing and quite revolutionary concept. This I could not get over.

Apart from the fact that the film concerned Russians and people bayonetting each other and glamorous women flouncing around in crinolines, I couldn't really follow the story of Part One much, but I loved it anyway. I spent the whole of the following week salivating with anticipation at the thought of returning to the cinema for Part Two, in which, as I recall, Audrey Hepburn looked even more beautiful than she had in Part One. Well, perhaps I had grown a few more hormones in those seven days. 'Natasha' was the name of the character she played. I promised myself that if I ever met a 'Natasha' when I grew up I would marry her.

Shortly after this experience my parents and I went to see *Butch Cassidy and the Sundance Kid* in the same cinema – was it the Adelphi perhaps? This wasn't as good as *War and Peace* because it was only in one part and it didn't feature Audrey Hepburn, or, indeed, any characters at all called Natasha or dressed in furry hats or bayonetting each other. But it was still pretty good.

The other cinema in Dun Laoghaire was the Pavilion, a vast, pastel-coloured, ornately-corniced, high-glamour building which was as quintessentially 50s as a little red Chevvy. (The Pavilion is now, sadly, also defunct, and is about to be turned into a yuppie apartment block.) You could see a film on a Saturday afternoon in the Pavilion for tenpence, and my brother and sisters and I often did. Many a marriage in the greater south Dublin area was saved, or at least prolonged, by the existence of the Pavilion cinema.

In school there was a film every Friday at seven o'clock in the hall. A nice priest called Father Al Flood was in charge of this. Every year, two or three boys were selected for film duty and one year myself and a friend, James 'Belly' Boland, were among those who got this amazingly privileged job. The position involved Father Flood driving us into town after school on a Friday in order to collect that night's film from the distributor's office, which, as far as I can remember, was just off Westland Row, and then driving us back to the school, where we would get the reels out of their big metal circular boxes and set up the projector and generally think we were really something.

The Friday night films were typically such fine, sensitive works as *The Guns Of Navarone*, *The Great Escape*, *Those Magnificent Men in their Flying Machines* and *Torah, Torah, Torah*, which is a deeply educational and multiculturally-useful film about the bombing of Pearl Harbor by the evil yellow atheistical menace. From time to time, Father Flood would tire of films about lunatics racing around in basket balloons and foreign bowzies being blown up by American soldiers, and for a few Friday nights there would be films with religious themes, such as *The Ten Commandments* and *Brother Sun, Sister Moon*. These were not nearly so much fun, although it was widely rumoured that several people had actually died during the making of *The Ten Commandments*. It was fun watching out for those bits.

Father Jarlath Dowling was another very nice priest. He taught music in my school. He actually lived in the music room, I seem to recall; his small bed, which always looked like it had been recently slept in by some kind of wild animal, was in a passageway just off the room where the trumpets and tubas and kettledrums were stored. He was fanatically interested in old movies. He had a pull-down screen and a rattling projector in the music room, and very often he would show us a Laurel and Hardy or Marx Brothers movie when we should have been listening to Beethoven or Brahms. He was a plump, passionate, fiery man with a bald head. Whenever he either lost his temper or burst out laughing for any length of time he would sweat heavily, and his face would go red and heat up, with the result that the sweat on his scalp would turn into steam. When this happened– and it happened not infrequently – it was quite an effect. He could have sold tickets for this and made a lot of dough.

I remember one time during a music class Father Dowling decided we really should see *A Night At The Opera*, which had the considerable virtue of combining his two great enthusiasms. The screen was pulled down, the chairs were pulled up, the curtains were drawn and off we went. Five minutes into the film Father Dowling, who was sitting just down the row from me, started to laugh. It was what comic books call a 'titter' at first, and then it grew to a 'chortle'. Shortly after this he began to guffaw and then to snort. He tried to control himself. He sat very still, his legs tightly crossed, his face red, the occasional apologetic cluck of mirth bursting forth from his massive frame. But it was no good. Before long he was rocking back and forth on his chair, slapping his thighs and actually honking with helpless unrestrained laughter. And then the poor man just lost it. He couldn't stop. What I can only describe as a *blast* of laughter exploded out of him. It sounded like one of his beloved trumpets being played by a lunatic. He howled. He bawled. He groaned. The Marx Brothers cantered across the screen and Father Dowling opened his mouth and roared and bellowed with laughter. He jumped to his feet and walked up and down the music room clutching his large stomach, laughing, big tears rolling down his chubby face. Thirty seconds later the entire class of nine-year-old boys was in utter hysterics. The principal must have heard the noise because he burst in shortly afterwards to find out what was going on. He glared astonished at Father Dowling, who was now openly sobbing with glee and leaning on a radiator with a hanky stuffed into his mouth, and then he glared at us, and then he glared up at the screen, where the Marx Brothers were now doing a dance. And then the principal started laughing. Which made Father Dowling laugh even more. And then the steam started coming from Father Dowling's head. Which made us nearly widdle with laughter. And so on. It was astonishing. My introduction to Marxism. To this day, it's probably the happiest memory I have of school, and, indeed, of the cinema.

Another movie recollection – less pleasurable, although more poignant: the first real date I ever had in my life involved the Forum Cinema in Glasthule, a large bag of popcorn, a lot of hope and deodorant and a very nice girl from Monkstown called Patricia Keegan who I had met in the Presentation College Disco, Glasthule ('Prez'), the previous Saturday night and who had beautiful hair. The film we went to see was *Midnight Express*, which, it turned out, was about an unfortunate American youth called Billy Hayes who gets imprisoned for twenty years in Turkey for smuggling drugs. The people who run the Turkish Tourist Board must have shot themselves when this film was released. Let me tell you, if you are trying to make a good impression, this is not a good movie to see on a first date. Poor Billy Hayes. Torture, gang rape, sodomy, nudity, squalor, filth, cockroaches, endless cursing and public masturbation are all very well, but if you want that kind of thing you'd really do better to stay at home. *Midnight Express* featured all those thought-provoking themes and more. Every five minutes, it seemed to me, Patricia emitted another feigned puking noise or plaintive wail of disgust and scowled at me like I was some sort of pervert for bringing her to this hideous gore-fest. The film climaxed with a scene of a man biting another man's tongue out and spitting it across a prison dining room in glorious technicolour slow motion. I will never forget the sound which issued forth from the darkness beside me at this point. It was the sound of Patricia Keegan going 'oh Jeeeeeeeeezus'. As I watched the tongue flying across the screen I somehow felt that the chances of my own tongue making any contact whatsoever with Patricia Keegan's later on in the evening were becoming pretty slim. And I was right, as it turned out.

She broke my heart when she dumped me. Every time I see *Midnight Express* I still think of her. And the funny thing is, after all these years I still reckon Billy Hayes got off lighter than me.

June Considine
Nesting in the Back Row

The supermarket stands on the site of the old Casino Cinema, at a junction where five roads meet and the pulse of traffic is never still. Every time I pass this place I look towards the beckoning posters advertising this week's special offers, and remember the days when a poster had the power to fill my heart with a fierce longing to witness what it promised. Childhood memories are like limpets: those we choose to retain cling to our minds, needing only a song, a few coded words or the site of a once-famous landmark to make them come to life in vivid detail.

Finglas in the mid-50s was only a speckle of shops and houses. Narrow roads linked to fields, stretching as far as the eye could see, and idle days spent with friends under the shadows of trees belonged to forever. But progress was snapping at our heels and one of its first manifestations was the appearance of the Casino Cinema.

We'd never seen anything like it – the black shining walls and doors of glass, the alluring posters of lean, rangy cowboys and beautiful women with breasts shaped like ice cream cones...

My mother was suspicious of the Casino. She muttered grimly about the goings-on of young people who should have better things to do at night than sit in a smoke-filled den of temptation. Her voice had that certain tone and I knew she was referring to the Back Row, two words that had the power to send older girls into a seizure of high-pitched giggling. I had to wait until *The Song of Bernadette* before my mother set aside her misgivings and decided that I would not be corrupted by the miracle of Lourdes.

Nothing had prepared me for the magic of that moment when I entered the cinema: the hushed darkness, the soft swinging seats, the swish of heavy curtains and the music reverberating around me. On the way home I was so overwhelmed with holiness that I stared fixedly into dark spaces in the hope of seeing an apparition.

From then on the Casino became part of my life. Permission was never granted easily, but that made the thrill even more intense when I was allowed to accompany my friends. It cost ninepence for the stalls and one and a penny for the balcony. For this we watched a double feature or one film accompanied by a cartoon, a travelogue feature and the Pathe News. We much preferred the double feature, especially if it was a horror combination like *The Night of the Living Dead* and *The Fall of the House of Usher*. At the end of the show we hid low in our seats in the hope of avoiding the usherette's torch. Sometimes we succeeded and got double value. More often we were rounded up and ordered out into daylight.

We were an uncritical audience, yet the abuse of the censor, whom we called the Axe Man, often left us howling with outrage. Many films were savaged beyond redemption, moving from scene to scene with total disregard for the story. In one film a young couple sat in the back seat of a car watching an open-air movie. When we saw them again she was crying on his shoulder.

'I'm expecting a...' she gasped.

'You can't be expecting a...!' he gasped back, his crew-cut wilting in shock. In the next scene he was heading out of town in his Chevvy. It was all very puzzling. We were a generation of innocents, weaned on strange stories of babies found under cabbage leaves, delivered with milk bottles or left in cots in convents by angels when no one was looking. But the Casino was slowly eroding this innocence.

The kissing scenes on the screen always seemed so much more dignified than the rustling, sighing, heaving, giggling manoeuvres in the infamous Back Row. The realisation that boys had other functions in life besides throwing popcorn over the balcony and roaring when the Bad Guy appeared was impossible to comprehend. It filled us with a mixture of horror and anticipation.

The seats in the Back Row were occupied by young woman in dirndl skirts and waspie belts, often dressed identically if they were friends and double-dating. Their boyfriends had corrugated waves in the front of their hair, and yellow narrow ties. We called them the Love Birds. We were the Love Bird Watchers. The LBWs.

It wasn't really cricket, but, seeing that nobody would talk to us about this mysterious rite of passage, we had to do our own research. We tried to sit as close to them as possible, to observe the action. But Love Birds were a secretive and aggressive breed, much given to verbal violence and threats of death if we strayed too close to their nests. But always in a low voice. The usherette, a guardian of morality, was ready to move in at the first sign of trouble. The piercing beam of her torch and the ringing command 'You two! Out!' were dreaded instructions which Love Birds would do anything to avoid.

I suppose they're grandparents today. Probably some of them shop in this supermarket that was once a cinema, pushing trolleys between rows of fresh and frozen foods, sampling slivers of ham and the newest easi-spread in the same spot where once they sampled other, more robust and memorable delights.

My limpet memory of the Casino is the sensation I carried with me on the way home from the cinema. I was the star. I walked in her shoes, swaying my hips and shoulders, my eyes smouldering, flashing, commanding. When I spoke my voice was a deep, purring drawl. No one seemed to notice that I was a different person. But that didn't matter. I was discovering the power of imagination; and living in it, even for a short while, opened the door into another world. It's a door which I have never wanted to close.

Patrick Bergin

I saw my first film, *King Richard III*, at the Regal or the Royal. My mother had taken me from my school, Loreto Convent Infants in St Stephen's Green, for the treat. To this day I can still hear Olivier's 'A horse, a horse, my kingdom for a horse'. I was to see *Moby Dick* with my brother Emmet around the same time, but somehow that day I ended up losing my sailing boat amongst the artificial bulrushes in one of the lovely circular ponds in St Stephen's Green and being chased out by the keeper as we tried to wade across to get it.

Our family moved out to Drimnagh where there were 'follower-uppers' at the Bosco Boys' Club on Saturday mornings, sometimes a Bowery Boys or a Mother Riley. But the bulk of my early cinema experience was in the Star Cinema Crumlin Road (later referred to as the 'Rats': 'star' spelled backwards). It was toffee-apples and smelly puddles round the back for the 9d seats. When there was a really good one on we were forced to sit crushed together, two in a seat, cheering our hero Audie Murphy in *To Hell and Back*. A cowboy or a fencing movie guaranteed streams of kids chasing each other across the Crumlin Road, around five o'clock of a Saturday and Sunday afternoon, with spears, swords, guns and bows and arrows.

On Saturday afternoons I went behind the Star cinema to Pearse Park to play soccer. Sunday afternoon was definitely picture-going time before the Wonderful World of Disney took over. I was given a shilling to go to the pictures – 9d for entrance, 1d up and 1d back on the bus.

One Sunday, my Mum having already given me my shilling, my Dad called me upstairs. He was having a snooze, and he asked me if I had got my shilling. Of course I lied through my teeth. That day I nearly broke my jaw on hard Cleeves Toffee, Black Jack and Silver Butterscotch (my favourite), and sickened myself on fizzy sherbet bags.

The Star showed up to six different films a week: two from Monday to Wednesday, another two from Thursday to Saturday, and a special Sunday night picture for courting couples. My last embrace of childhood was being taken to the final show on Wednesday night to see *Tom Thumb*. I was desperate to see it; my mother asked the usherette to let me in for the night show, and she came to collect me afterwards.

Maybe I didn't want to grow up, but grow up I did. Soon I was going to the Star on Monday nights, when it became the scene of an amazing courting spectacle. Between the end of the first film and the beginning of the second almost everybody stood up and 'went for a walk'. Walking around the aisles, we identified likely couples of girls to sit beside, in front of, or behind, so that we might pinch, annoy or drop the hand on them to see if we might get lucky. A 'wear' was not unusual.

If you were lucky enough to have money you bought a pack of Tayto or Perri crisps and drowned out the first minute and a half of the big picture with a cacophony of crunching crisps and crisp packets.

Violence was an increasing problem when venturing into other territories; trips to 'the 'Core' in Inchicore or the Stella in Walkinstown, or even to the Rialto or the Leinster at Dolphin's Barn (which legend had it was sinking into a swamp), took courage. I was 'claimed' there many a time.

Sex and violence were everywhere: in *Jailhouse Rock, The Blackboard Jungle, Sinbad the Sailor, Hercules Unchained*, in Elvis movies and in Burt Lancaster Circus movies. The poster for *Cleopatra* could fuel a Sherman.

My favourite films were the 'B' movies: *The Fiend that Walked the West, Terror of the Tongs* and Broderick Crawford's *Joe Macbeth*.

I remember bawling my eyes out, having wandered unknowingly into the Green cinema to see *How Green was my Valley*. I was fascinated by the title *Greengage Summer*, which showed there also. For a while it seemed as if only films with 'green' in the title were shown there. I loved the Green. I loved the smell of it. We were moving back into town.

The Deluxe became a favourite on Sunday afternoon. 1/3d upstairs – I saw *The Magnificent Seven* seven times. I saw every Elvis movie up to *Roustabout* and finally abandoned my loyalty after his disastrous version of *Frankie and Johnny*. But Ann-Margret in *Viva Las Vegas* and Juliet Prowse in *G.I. Blues*... Then there were the epics: *Ben Hur* at the Ambassador seemed to take up the corner of O'Connell Street and Parnell Street for years. I was transported by the first moving personification of Jesus Christ in *King of Kings*. We were taken by the school to see *The Robe*, which was so long it had an interval. We were overawed. *How the West was Won* was new at Cinerama. *Dr Zhivago* occupied the Metropole for another eternity. I was so impressed I bought a long green army/FCA coat from my next-door neighbour and had it dyed brown so I could be the first head in Dublin with a Dr Zhivago coat. Then there was the exotic: *Africa Addio, Mondo Cane* and *Mondo Bazaar* at the Astor.

When I got really sophisticated I took my Juliet to *Un Homme et une Femme* (twice), to *Blow-Out*, to Bette Davis in *The Anniversary* (not a good idea) and of course to Zeffirelli's *Romeo and Juliet*. My Juliet was more beautiful than Olivia Hussey when she took her glasses off; however, she kept them on and saw right through me.

Then I got a date with the coolest, most beautiful girl in Dublin and managed to get tickets from a tout on O'Connell Bridge to the chaos of Sunday night courtship.

The excitement was killing.

They were for the Metropole, *Carry On Screaming*. People did scream. I was speechless. Corpsed beside my beauty.

The night – an apologetic ache.

In fact I was supposed to go out with her sister. So much for fidelity.

Still, I quite fancied the vampish Fenella Fielding in her red velvet gown – all was not lost. I was fourteen years old – I had fantasy – I had the movies!

Maeve Binchy
Where Anything Could Happen

I loved going to the pictures in the 1950s, and there were three cinemas in Dun Laoghaire. The Adelphi on George's Street, the main street, is a block of offices now; the Pavilion down near the sea is nothing yet, just standing broken down waiting for something to happen to it; and the Astoria, which was more Glasthule really, is still a grand cinema called the Forum.

On Saturday afternoons all the girls from school would meet outside whichever one we were going to – we had school on Saturday in those days, and I remember coming home for lunch and all the other girls saying 'Thank God we'll be able to get out of school uniform this afternoon'. I used to say that, even though I didn't really look any better in things that weren't my school uniform. I actually liked my thick green school skirt, but I never admitted it because it sounded abnormal.

And popcorn came in during those days. I hated it – I still do – but I ate buckets of it because everyone else thought it was great.

And every single Saturday my father would say 'Wouldn't a nice walk along the pier be better than being cooped up in a stuffy cinema?' And every single Saturday I said that maybe I'd have a nice walk on the pier next week, and he always gave me the money with a sigh.

And we used to giggle a lot and hate the love scenes and particularly hate the dream dance scenes. We would talk through them.

And when there were close-up kisses, all kinds of Rough Boys would shout out 'Ugh! Ugh!' and everyone would scream with laughter, and then an usher with a torch would flash it along the rows so it quietened us.

There were occasionally grownups who liked kisses and dream dance sequences.

And I loved it when the lion roared because like everyone in the world we *knew* he was from our zoo. And we loved the man with muscles hitting the gong, and the Movietone News and the trailers, and we hated the documentaries from the National Film Board of Canada.

And I fell in love at the pictures – with a horrible young man who wasn't worthy of me and who invited me one Saturday afternoon to see an Audrey Hepburn film, which was a penance for a plump teenager, and then wanted to meet me inside, the louse, so that I couldn't parade him up and down in front of my school friends.

And then I fell properly in love with Marlon Brando and wrote to him cheerfully for years telling him to come to Ireland and change his lifestyle. He did come to Ireland later, like nearly forty years later, but then it was too late for me. And for him too, as it turned out.

But I always look back on those Saturday afternoons with great happiness. Turning your back on a healthy walk on the pier and going into the smell of popcorn and cheese-and-onion, and getting transported off to a world where nobody looked like us and where anything could happen to anyone...

Myles Dungan

An unenlightened upbringing in a small town, followed by five years in a professionally unenlightened boarding school, ensured that my early exposure to the transformation of 'darkness into light' was as limited as that of the cast of *The Song of Bernadette* to VD. Thus the first film I ever saw offered a double dose of Hayley Mills in *The Parent Trap* (along with Maureen O'Hara). I can only assume that I pestered my elders with questions about how she managed to play identical twin sisters. I certainly would not have bothered them with queries about the semiological significance of the dual personality or the techniques used to create some of the *Day for Night* effects. (As I was unfamiliar with French at the age of ten, the phrase 'nuit Américaine' wouldn't have entered my lexicon.)

Not that it had much chance to: my early movie-going career came to an abrupt end when *Thunderball* came to town, with Sean Connery at his hirsute best as James Bond. Hissing at the villain, I split my sides when Bond impaled a baddie on the tip of a harpoon, with the casual quip 'I think he got the point'. My mother wasn't similarly amused. Assailed by doubts about the suitability of an adaptation of the work of such a libertine as Ian Fleming, she went along the following night. The result? 'NEVER AGAIN' was I to lighten the inside of the picture house.

Two decades later, however, *Thunderball* was remade as *Never Say Never Again*, with a less hirsute (but considerably sexier) Sean Connery in the title role. Attending the Dublin launch of the film as a guest of the distribution company, I mused on the futility of trying to keep children out of cinemas.

Nothing would give me more pleasure than to go on and write about a subsequent period of clandestine film-going during which I was mesmerised by the first screening of Truffaut's *Les Quatre Cents Coups* in Kells, Co. Meath. Sadly, the truth was I went to boarding school, hardly even seeing a TV, never mind a cinema screen.

Once let loose in Dublin, though, staying in my older brother's flat, I went to the movies on my last two days of freedom from school. Here was a golden opportunity, a chance to become a true cinéaste. Instead I chose to go and see *The Sound of Music* in Talbot Street, immediately falling madly in love with Julie Andrews. (It would never have worked!) The following day offered another chance to see something informative or uplifting. Instead I went back to *The Sound of Music* and wondered how I could ever get to meet my dearest Julie.

Back on permanent remand in boarding school, I would occasionally earn a temporary release on the pretext of getting my eyes tested or going to the dentist (my teeth are a mass of fillings due to my devotion to the cinematic arts). A few rare Saturday afternoons were spent in the only cinema in Cavan town (perhaps I'm just sentimentalising its powers of attraction, but I think it was called the Magnet). Here I met up, once again, with Mr Connery, this time in a Western called *Shalako*. I was far more interested in his female companion, as this odd concoction of 'John Ford meets Oscar Wilde' afforded me my first cinematic encounter with Brigitte Bardot. My virgin-pure unilateral love affair with Julie Andrews ended on the spot and I discovered lust. (Although oddly, my first actual juvenile sexual encounter in a cinema – my first grope, in other words – was at a performance of *Bambi* – which is a lot like necking during *The Nun's Story*.)

I will say one thing for my schooldays. About as regularly as Cavan winning the All-Ireland championship (and I managed to post-date the glory days), a film would be shown on the clapped-out college projector on Sunday evenings. Mostly these would be quasi-religious and uplifting, but at least one subversive and uplifting picture slipped through.

It was there, one Sunday night, that I sat open-mouthed through *Dr Strangelove*, and learned to stop worrying and love the bomb!

THE FOLLIER-UPPERS

Bryan Murray
Pigeons at the Feeno

I was born and brought up in Islandbridge, by the Phoenix Park. Sarah Place was the name of the road – a row of white-washed cottages – and I was born there in the late 50s. We used to play 'cowboys and Indians' in the street, and 'spin the bottle' and 'kick the can'.

There came a time in my childhood when the notion of being allowed to go to the cinema was suddenly threatened. I was about nine at the time. I had been nagging my mother, but she was very much against it because I was young and at my age you didn't go anywhere which demanded a bus journey, even then. The nearest cinema, which was quite far away, was the Phoenix cinema. It was known as the 'Feeno', in the Dublin way of abridging everything. The cinema was a long bus journey – all the way to Parkgate Street, along by Kingsbridge and down the Quays.

Eventually, after I had beseeched my mother, she relented one Sunday afternoon and it was agreed that the gang would go to the Feeno. This was an awfully big adventure. I had no idea what to expect. All I knew was that it was fantastic. This was the first time I had been out without my parents – out with the lads. We were each given a shilling – sixpence into the pictures, fourpence for the bus fares and tuppence to spend. The gang set off for the bus stop. There was Hammer Keegan, the leader, Bernard White, Shamie Boland and Willy Baneham. We're the lads, but there's one fella joining us called Redmond and he's a demon. We're not allowed to hang around with him. On the way to the bus stop he has the great suggestion that we walk to town and back and then we'll have sixpence to spend. This was breaking all the rules... The adventure was only beginning.

At the shop beside the cinema there was always a mill of kids. We went into the shop and instead of having only tuppence to spend, we were rich with our sixpences. You could get two marshmallow mice – a pink one and a white one – for a penny; and one sailor's chew for a penny, but you'd be chewing on it for days – I think they were made of rubber; and two gobstoppers for a penny. I'd never had that amount of money to spend all in one go, so this was living dangerously. Not only did we all spend the tuppence we had, but we spent both bus fares – so now we were stranded.

Off into the pictures – we don't even know which film is showing, but that doesn't matter. This is the tuppenny rush, and inside the lights are still on and the entire place is teeming with kids from all over and no adults. This is our first experience of the pictures – a kind of rite of passage. Of course, the Feeno was a flea-pit. They used to say that if you went in a cripple – you'd come out walking! Lots of argy-bargy, scream-ing and shouting.

I'm sitting near the end of the row beside this guy who's wearing a bomber jacket (which was a bit strange on a summer's day but...). The lights go down. The follier-upper begins and it's Batman, dangling on the edge of a cliff, and we're there watching and chewing – the world is our oyster in Dublin in 1958. The fellow with the bomber jacket is there and I hear strange noises coming from the jacket.

About ten minutes into the film, the guy unzips his jacket and out into the darkness fly two pigeons, who dash blindly around, totally disorien-tated and getting caught in the glare of the silver beams of light. They fly wildly against the screen, dazed and confused. The cinema is a riot at this stage, and in my innocence, I think this is what cinema is – I'm up cheering, and shouting 'Yahoo! Go! Go! Go!' A light is flashed in my face – I'm grabbed by the neck, dragged out amid yells and accusations from my mates who are guilty by association. 'It wasn't me. It wasn't me.'

Gobstoppers are lost, marshmallow mice are mangled underfoot and we are thrown out of the Feeno, into the daylight, less than fifteen minutes after we'd arrived. So this was the pictures – the great adventure – over. And we had the rest of the afternoon to walk home.

John McMahon

The rather drab parish hall in Ballyheigue was a far cry from the picture palaces of the cities – a long narrow building, with benches towards the front and somewhat more comfortable seats at the back. Every week, however, it was transformed by the power of the projector. The excite-ment would grow as the film reels arrived in the bus from Tralee. It wasn't unusual to find that a reel was missing, or even that a different film had arrived – although this could be to our advantage. The projectionist would collect it and bring it to his 'projection box'. Thereafter followed the ritual of taking the reels from the cans and preparing them for the projector. No one was allowed near during this process – it was privilege enough to be allowed to watch.

I remember few of the feature films, but the joys and thrillers of the follier-uppers still remain with me. The hero could be a cowboy, like Hopalong Cassidy, or the Lone Ranger, or even a London policeman – Whoever-it-was of the Yard pursuing London's villains in his black Wolsley police car, trying to solve the crime within the allotted time. Every week we waited with bated breath to see if our hero had survived that almighty leap across the chasm, the ambush that had been set, or whatever. To our relief every week he triumphed, only to face yet another trial at the end of the fifteen minutes, and again we were held in suspense for another week. This rather basic technique kept us coming back week after week.

Very occasionally, we were treated to a visit to a 'real' cinema in Tralee – a choice between the Ashe Memorial, the Theatre Royal and the Picturedrome. The tension of the chariot race in *Ben Hur* was seen in awe-inspiring cinemascope in one of these. Bible epics were a must – at last our parents could believe that the cinema had some positive benefits.

Mind you, my most memorable film is the one I never saw. At boarding school in Killarney during the 1960s we were treated to a film once a month or so, on Sunday afternoon. One Saturday afternoon, a group of us decided to slip into Killarney against school rules, and of course we were caught on the way back. The punishment: no film the following afternoon. I can still recall my feelings of injustice as we walked around and around the quadrangle with the trumpet solo from *The Legion's Last Patrol* ringing out clearly from the blacked-out study hall.

Frank Feely

They were never cinemas, when I was a kid, they were picture houses. If we were asked to list the most important people in the community, the cinema usher would have been high on the list. He was God. Queuing up, the dreaded words were 'three seats left' when you were fourth in the queue.

Friday was the day when they changed the billboard posters indicating what was on next week. On surmounting the summit of Harold's Cross Bridge, cycling home from school at Synge Street, I would immediately look at the new poster in the distance to see what was on next week in the Classic, my local cinema. What lofty names they gave my local picture-houses – Stella, Apollo, Princess, Classic, Rialto, Camden and Theatre De Luxe.

Each of the Dublin cinemas had its own characteristics. While the seats were narrower than they are in modern cinemas and the cheaper ones were very often wooden benches, we never complained of discomfort. The Stella in Rathmines is my earliest memory of the cinema, with its – luxury of luxuries – fountain at the front bathed in green light. The Camden, low down on the hierarchy of respectable cinemas, had the special characteristic of the screen being over the door through which you entered, so the self-conscious entrants had to run the gamut of the hundreds of staring eyes of the facing audience. The Sundrive (could you really get in for a jam jar? They used to say you could, but I never saw anyone producing one) lined up its prospective customers alongside the Poddle River and the cash office was behind a door, halfway down the side of the cinema. This was only for matinées – at night the adults went in through the front door. However, at the matinées on a Saturday or Sunday afternoon, we would sit expectantly waiting until the queue was fully disgorged into the cinema. The woman cashier would lock up the cash office, put the cash box under her arm and walk up the cinema to the cheers of the waiting youngsters. I'm sure she hated that moment every week.

One thing I always associated with the Sundrive was the practice of hurling the cardboard tops of milk bottles, about an inch and a half in diameter, up through the projector beam if the film became boring. It required a special technique to throw it up high enough, but the reward was a flash of light on the cardboard top as it spun through the beam. Often the film was stopped and an usher sent down to seek out the offender, only to find a sea of innocent faces.

And what of the films? We were big into cowboys. For a while the Corinthian Cinema on Eden Quay earned the name of 'the Ranch' because of its propensity to show cowboy films. The biggest hero of them all was Hopalong Cassidy (or William Boyd, to give him his real name). The reputation of another well-known cowboy, Gene Autrey, suffered from the fact that he actually kissed girls, and even worse, he sang. Hoppy would never do that! Years later I remembered the young Gene Autrey, handsome, slim and immaculately dressed in white, when I met the real thing in Dublin – an old man but still charming. I particularly remembered him as a young man bringing the traffic in Dublin to a standstill when he made a personal appearance in the Theatre Royal.

Then there were the follower-uppers – *The Clutching Hand*, *Flash Gordon Conquers The Universe* and *Winners of the West*. They cheated like hell! One week you would go home convinced that the hero was dead since he had fallen off a train travelling at speed along the edge of a canyon. The following week we'd pick up the story at the same point. Your hero, whom you last saw in mid-air, falling to his death, was now caught by a tree on the edge of the track as he fell. You swore that the tree wasn't there the previous week – but then how could you be certain? It was a whole week ago.

John Quinn
Off-Cuts

The earliest memories I have of cinema are of a fit-up cinema with a leaky roof in a field of foot-high grass... There was a 'follier-upper' called *The Clutching Hand* and it terrified us every week. Then there was Sikey Dunne's Picture-Show. When James Cagney died, I wrote a poem about him and about Sikey Dunne's show.

When the fit-up moved on, the great thrill was to find little off-cuts of film in the long grass (censored bits? or chopped-out bits when the film broke?). We would hold them up to the sun and try to figure out what they signified. To find a sword-fight ranked way above a soppy kiss!

We lived in a small sleepy midlands village – Ballivor, Co. Meath. The nearest real cinema was the Royal in Trim. It was a source of unending joy to be summoned on a Sunday evening with the words 'We're going to the pictures'. 'The Cuckoo Waltz' greeted us as we entered. No wet grass underfoot or drips from above here. Plush red seats and a thick carpet...

The lights dimmed, the music faded and we were in another world. Two and a half or three hours of solid entertainment: a newsreel, a cartoon or two, a travelogue (or, better still, Joe McDoak's) and the 'big picture'. We hoped it wouldn't be what my father called 'a woman's picture' – but rather 'a gangster' or 'a cowboy'. We were never in any danger of corruption by celluloid – on the journey home my mother led us in the family rosary.

Later we moved to Rathmines in Dublin. Cine-utopia! The Theatre De Luxe in Camden Street and the Princess and the Stella in Rathmines were all within a ten-minute walk. Sadly, only the Stella survives today. The Princess, or 'Prinner', as it was locally known, was a rough enough place – it was a wise move to go for the one-and-ninepenny seats upstairs rather then the one-and-threes below. Still, you always got good value in the Prinner – usually a double feature.

This was the 50s – pre-television days when, if you could afford it, you could go to a matinée in town in the afternoon (and sit through it twice if you liked it) and then go to the local at night. This was the 50s – when touts did a roaring trade up and down O'Connell Street selling black market tickets for the Sunday night performances. My own personal record was three films in one day – I remember kicking off with a charity showing of *Calamity Jane* in the Adelphi on a Saturday morning (admission one shilling!).

This was the 50s – when the cinema was a labour-intensive business. A burly commissionaire at the door, two cashiers, three or four usherettes – who flashed their torches at troublemakers who shouted 'BEHIND YA!' just when the baddie was about to strike – and two ice-cream girls who stood self-consciously with their trays under the spotlights during the interval.

As an impressionable teenager, I was totally smitten by a film called *The Kidnappers* – the story of two young boys who go to live with their grandparents (the austere Duncan Macrae and the charming Jean Anderson) in Nova Scotia. Grandfather won't let them have a pet so they 'borrow' a baby and hide it in the woods. Wonderful performances from the boys, Jon Whitely and especially Vincent Winter, who stole the film. I thought it was wonderful – must have seen it six, eight, ten times... What ever happened to you, boys? I never heard of you again.

Memories? My young life story could be traced through the cinema. Dodging tomahawks at a 3-D Western in the Corinthian, falling in love with Grace Kelly, straining to hear the dialogue every time a train rumbled past the New Electric in Talbot Street, wishing I could be cool like Richard Widmark, being absolutely knocked out by the stereo sound of the dancehall scene in *West Side Story* when I walked into the Savoy (the real Savoy, the old cavernous Savoy) – and boy, did I sit though that twice.

And still... And still...

Nothing can replace the magic of finding a strip of celluloid in the trampled dank grass when the fit-up moved on – and holding it up to the sunlight. Hey, look! I got Roy Rogers – and Trigger!

PG – PARENTAL GUIDANCE

Maxine Brady

I grew up in Lurgan, Co. Armagh, a town without a cinema. I remember four trips to the pictures over a seventeen-year period, until I left home. When I mentioned to my mother that I was writing this article and castigated her for not driving the ten miles to the cinema in Banbridge more often, she argued that she had. But when I pointed out that many of the movies she remembers were seen on video, years after their release, she conceded the point. In a way I can understand why she was so reluctant to go to the pictures more often. Blockbusters sometimes meant queues too long to have any hope of getting in. Why make a ten-mile drive just to disappoint excited kids in the back of the car?

Of course things have changed somewhat. Lurgan now has a four-screen cinema complex attached to a bowling alley, snack-bar, bar and night-club. But in the 70s and 80s it was a rare treat that had to be planned with military precision. The whole outing had to be timed to try and miss the queues, so weekends were out. Weekdays were deemed more accessible, which meant exhausted children at school next morning, leaving home at least two hours before the showing and probably still queuing since the Banbridge theatre was the only one for miles around. (With the honourable exception, of course, of Portadown Community Centre – a smelly, cold and uncomfortable hall, where you could see movies months after everyone else, and where you could buy a packet of cheese-and-onion crisps with a bottle of orangeade. There was no pop-corn at our movie outings.)

The first movie I remember seeing was Disney's *Bambi*. I can remember becoming dreadfully upset when Bambi's mother was murdered before my young and innocent eyes. Quite how profoundly it affected me was brought home by a trip to Finland in 1987 for a conference. In Finland, reindeer is food. Finns regularly eat smoked reindeer as a starter, with salad. Every time I saw it on the menu, or another delegate ate it in my presence, I was assaulted by memories of Bambi. I simply couldn't stand the idea of consuming that cute, cuddly fawn.

My other memories, such as they are, are not in chronological order, since my memory leaves a lot to be desired.

Jaws II was a sop to my sister and me. We had wanted to see *Jaws*, but were deemed too young. My parents had seen the original, and throughout the showing of *Jaws II*, as we jumped in our seats, they informed us that the first movie was better. In retribution I went home and read the original book, which was more scary than either movie.

Star Wars was an unusual choice. Told by my male peers at school that it was a boy's movie, I immediately demanded to go, so that I could talk about Darth Vader and Luke Skywalker. Since my father also wanted to see *Star Wars*, we went. It is perhaps one of my more embarrassing memories.

My sister was very young and the theatre was packed as usual. My parents and sister sat in one row, I sat in the row in front. My sister, bored out of her mind, spent the whole time charging up and down the aisle, shooting people. Since money was not in plentiful supply in those days, my mother was frugal with the refreshments. She brought with her a six-pack of crisps from Dunnes and a huge bottle of Coke. The Coke was passed along. There were two other kids with us, both boys, both younger. The youngest fell asleep; the older boy, who is now an aspiring actor in London, was successful in getting soggy crisps into the bottle of Coke, which made me feel nauseated and meant that Thomas got to drink it all.

This was no big deal as far as I was concerned, but hoisting up a huge bottle of Coke for everyone behind me to see silhouetted against the screen was a major embarrassment, so I pretended I was with the couple next to me and not with my family.

But of all the movies we went to see, *Grease* was perhaps the most enjoyable and memorable. I still watch it at Christmas when they show it on television. I can still sing along with all the songs, and when USI held parties at Congress, Christmas or the end of the academic year, many of us could not only sing along, but do the dances as well.

Quite a few of us went that night – my mother, my aunt, my sister, my five-year-old cousin and two friends. We arrived at the cinema to a queue that appeared to be miles long. My mother wanted to go home, but a group of wailing teenagers convinced her to stay. We had literally got to the top of the queue when the House Full sign went up. Having queued for two hours already, we decided to wait for the second showing. My mother and aunt retired to the pub.

We queued for hours and when we finally got in we were ecstatic. The younger kids fell asleep and we didn't get home until almost midnight, but it was worth it to us.

As we got older, parents stopped taking us to the pictures, and boyfriends took over. Even then it was still a major undertaking. If a boyfriend had a car, it was often easier and quicker to go to Belfast, thirty miles away, to see a movie rather than queue in Banbridge .

I've been to the cinema quite a lot lately. My daughter has just reached the age when she can sit through a showing eating her popcorn and ice-cream. For her it's a normal event if there's a suitable film on. (Though she still doesn't understand why she can't see the dinosaurs in *Jurassic Park*.)

It's when I sit in the matinée showings and see the wonder on the faces of children that I realise what I missed. And of course friends tell me about their Saturday afternoons at the flicks when they threw lollipops and popcorn at each other. But they didn't have the excitement we had at the end of a movie. Cinemas in Northern Ireland play the British National Anthem at the end of every movie. When we went to the pictures as kids, the greatest thrill of all was charging out of the theatre before the National Anthem, to the disgust of staff and parents. To us, leaving before the anthem was finished was not only a statement of Catholic identity, but a challenge to authority. And while these days I'll sit in the theatre until after the anthem, I can still remember the thrill of hoping my mother didn't grab hold of me as I joined the heaving throng of Catholics, bullying their way into the fresh air, making their statement, as though to stand for *God Save the Queen* would undermine our nationalism.

Sandy Fitzgerald
Yo-Yos and Hula-Hoops

Cinema-going peaked in Dublin during the 50s. Each catchment area had one or more cinemas holding up to one thousand people. Within a mile radius of our family home you had the Bohemian (locally known as the 'Bo'), the opulent State Cinema in Phibsborough, or the boisterous kids in the Cabra Grand. For your money you got a newsreel, a 'B' picture (usually a serial called a 'follower-upper') and the main feature. The programme changed twice a week and was sometimes accompanied by a live act such as 'Johnny and his Magic Yo-yo' which was no more than a promotion for some fad or other (I also remember hula-hoop demonstrations) but great entertainment nonetheless. Couple all of this with your sweets and your street fights afterwards, and you come up with the best afternoon ever.

My father was an avid movie-goer, while my mother could take it or leave it. So it must have been my father who persuaded her that a day out would be good for us all, my parents and me. I can't see her bubbling with enthusiasm, considering I was just three years old and a hyperactive toddler at that. She reluctantly agreed, but gave dire warnings that we were wasting our money and that by the time the Movietone Cock crowed I would be crying and struggling to disappear among the half-eaten Trigger bars and Bon Bon wrappers on the floor.

The Cabra Grand was chosen on the basis that this screaming child could be frog-marched home within five minutes and given a proper thrashing. I remember nothing about the film except for the fact that my mother never tired of expressing her amazement that I sat through the whole programme without a sound, mesmerised by the screen. I never lost that sense of awe in the flickering image. The 'Bo', the State and the Cabra Grand have long since gone, but the multiplex still attracts me to its darkened recesses. Although I still await the return of Johnny and his magic yo-yo.

Mary Banotti

I grew up on the north side of Dublin and I can place our house on Stiles Road as being equidistant between the Fairview Cinema ('The Faro') and the Killester Cinema ('The Killer'). My exposure to the cinema when I was very young was particularly special. Owing to the risks of filming in England, many of the British cinema companies came to Ireland to film during the war. My father was an actor, and many times when I was very young, he seemed to disappear for a few days and come back with little presents for us. He took part in many of the Pinewood cinema movies shot in the forties – *I See a Dark Stranger*, and *Captain Boycott* – so we always had an almost proprietorial attitude towards the cinema. To this day I feel particularly proud and quite emotional when I see great films such as *Odd Man Out* and remember that our family had a small part in their creation.

Another rather bizarre film I remember from when I was very young also had a family connection. My aunt, Nora O'Mahony (later immortalised as Godmother in *Wanderly Wagon*) took part in a film intended to draw the nation's attention to the fact that germs lodged in cracked cups, and I was invited by my glamorous actress aunt to come to a screening. She played the part, if I remember correctly, of a somewhat slatternly waitress who put the cups on the table in a cheap café with her fingers stuck in them and a large crack evident in the cup. The waitress did not enjoy her job, and had a sneering expression on her face as the middle-class lady in a hat pointed out the dangers of germs and the need for better hygiene. Subsequently I heard that this film was a breakthrough – the first health education film ever made in this country.

Garret Fitzgerald

Around 1934 I remember ringing up my father in the Dáil to badger him into allowing me to go to a film about St Therese in the Bray picture house. Permission was granted. Suspecting it wouldn't be forthcoming, I didn't even seek permission when, aged thirteen, I went to *Dracula* and *Frankenstein* in the Dun Laoghaire picture house.

Eibhear Walshe
Transported

I recall two cinemas in Waterford: the Savoy and the Regina. There was also one called the Rex, but my experience was mainly at the Savoy. Memory suggests that it was considered an elegant place and had a Grill upstairs.

I remember my first trip to the cinema, when I was about five. My parents brought my brother and me to see *Lady and the Tramp* – this was in the year it came out, 1967 – and it was a complete disaster. I cried all the way home, remembering the rats in the film, and my brother was in a similar state of distress. This experience of being transported, whether for fun or fear, remains the key attraction of cinema for me. I used to be afraid of the cinema – a kind of fear of the dark, I suppose.

As I grew older, I was taken to the pictures sometimes by my aunts, who were just a bit older than I, or sometimes by my friend's father. I remember having an altercation with him over a choice of film – we were relishing the promise of racing, costume and spectacle in *Ben Hur*, while he was insisting that we would love James Bond. The biblical elements of *Ben Hur* appealed to me as a devout altar boy, perhaps.

When on holidays in Rosslare, I had to endure the worst of cinema experiences: spaghetti Westerns were projected with wavy soundtracks and scratchy prints. I disliked this almost as much as I disliked the sadism of those films. Ennio Morricone's musical score was totally lost on me.

As a teenager, cinema was a social option. I remember that I did choose to go and see *Saturday Night Fever* especially. Looking back now, it seems to me to be a more sophisticated film than I had thought at the time. John Travolta's rituals of grooming and preening conferred a legitimacy on men's attention to their looks. It gave permission to men, in a way.

Cinema can do that because it has that power to transport us. While my early experiences were tinged with fear of being in the dark, which is why I never went alone, now I like going alone.

STAR CAST

Hugh Leonard
The Bit-Players

When I was small, my mother took me to the pictures in Dun Laoghaire every Monday and Friday, and my father came with us on Sundays. My mother favoured the dingy little Picture House – known as the Bughouse – in George's Street. The Pavilion on the sea front was grander, but not even for Randolph (we called him 'Randaloph') Scott, Joel McCrea, Buck Jones, and Richard Dix, all in the same film, would she brave the east wind that scythed across the harbour and pursued us up Marine Road to the tram stop.

I vividly remember the Picture House. If you peered through the box-office grill, you saw a wall decorated with stills from the 1929 part-talkie version of *Showboat*, starring Joseph Schildkraut and Laura La Plante. You entered the cinema itself by a door beneath and to one side of the screen, so that if the film was already playing you walked up the aisle backwards in case you might miss an instant of it. The name of the head usher was Drummond; behind his back, we called him 'Ace' after the hero of a thirteen-part serial (or follower-upper), Ace Drummond.

The programme changed on Mondays and Thursdays, with a double-bill and the serial on Sundays. One Friday, my mother and I rolled up on a Friday afternoon as usual, to discover that Monday's film, *The Lives of a Bengal Lancer*, had been retained by public demand. We had, of course, seen it earlier in the week. To pay to see the same film twice was, for her, a fearful extravagance, but after agonizing for all of a minute, she said 'Oh, well, it was exciting!' and pushed our two fourpences under the brass box office grill. (When the government brought in entertainment tax in the early 1930s, she point-blank refused to pay it. She shoved fourpence at the cashier as before and – then and for ever after – marched in to take her usual seat in what were now the sixpennies.)

As you grew older, you recognised that each of the major studios had its own style. MGM shimmered with a quality that came as much from the stars – Gable, Crawford, Garbo, Beery, the Barrymores and Loy – as from the Rolls-Royce look of the sets. Films made at Paramount had a soft-focus look that matched the frothiness of such comedies as *Love Me Tonight, Midnight* and *Trouble in Paradise* – its star director, Ernst Lubitsch, said: 'I've been to Paris, France, and I've been to Paris, Hollywood. Paris, Hollywood, is better.'

I came to like Warner Bros. best of all. The sets were cheap and used shadows instead of walls; the exteriors seemed drab and sunless, and the film stock was grainy; but Warners had the best bit players in Hollywood.

In the 30s and 40s, type-casting was a fine art. Louis Jean Heidt and Eddie Quillan were the eternal losers; Margaret Hamilton, Almira Sessions and the superbly named Anita Sharpe Bolster were busybodies; Clem Bevans and Charley Grapewin were grizzled old-timers. It was a cinematic version of instant coffee: you simply took a bit player, added a film camera, and a character was there, ready-brewed. It saved so much time that it was a rare film that ran for more than eighty minutes.

When I speak of bit players, I do not mean the giants – Walter Brennan, Edward Arnold, Beulah Bondi and such. Rather, I think of faces that only a film maniac like myself could put a name to. Think of a Warners prison film starring James Cagney, and you will see Joseph Downing or Paul Fix as the shiv-wielding informer. Paul Guilfoyle and John Gallaudet were squealers, Alan Baxter was the psychopath con, and Ben Weldon and Edward Pawley were simply asking to have their ears pinned back by Cagney's arch-enemy, Bogart.

As the head of the parole board, Moroni Olsen was integrity itself; Joseph Crehan, who often played Ulysses S. Grant, was the tough warden; while John Litel, a model of probity, was the DA. Dick Rich was a brutal warder, and Ed Brophy and Joseph Sauer (later Sawyer) and Warren Hymer were dimwits. On visiting day, you might glimpse the hard-bitten Iris Adrian, Isabel Jewell, or the hardest-boiled blonde in films, Veda Ann Borg.

There were thousands of them. Donald Meek, like Chester Clute, was as timid as his name. Dick Elliot, fat and Stetsoned, was an out-of-towner. A patent on drunkenness was held by Arthur Houseman and Jack Norton, who never took a drink. Frank Orth was as immutably a bartender as his real-life wife, the Belgian actress Anne Codee, was a vivacious Parisienne. Franklin Pangborn dithered, Walter Catlett boggled and Raymond Walburn blustered.

Here I am, unable to remember the name or even the face of the lady next to whom I sat at last night's dinner party; and yet I can still see Douglas (sometimes Douglass) Dumbrille as Israel Hands in *Treasure Island* and Erik Rhodes as the professional co-respondent ('Your wife is-a safe weet Tonetti, he prefers-a spaghetti!') in *The Gay Divorcée*. And how often have I seen an elegant lady named Bess Flowers, a legend even in her time, as the 'queen of the dress extras'.

Perhaps not one of this great host of players ever earned more than a couple of hundred dollars a film. Each one played virtually the same tiny role – 'a cough and a spit' is the showbiz term – until he or she died. And yet they gave modest but enduring delight.

The voice of reason tells me that I have wasted my years remembering these long-departed shadows. And yet another voice, far wiser, tells me that perhaps to remember pleasure given by others is ourselves to be remembered. Which is codology. I simply can't forget them.

Dermot Bolger

O'Connell Street is packed, the crowds crossing from side to side oblivious to the hooting lines of cars. Long snakes form outside the cinemas. A busker plays *Love, Love me Do*. Inside the darkness of the large picture palace they watch James Garner in his officer's uniform confronting Julie Andrews and Joyce Grenfell. The cinema echoes with shouts and catcalls, the usher's torch bobs across the rows. They agree it's not as good as *My Fair Lady* or *Goldfinger*.

Bob Quinn
Great Movie Disasters

For me the difference between cinema-going as a child and as an adult is this: as a child I fell in love with the heroine, as an adult I fell in lust with her.

My relationship with Snow White was pure, passionate and completely unselfish. I wanted to die for her, there and then, at the matinée in the Savoy. As I couldn't – I was only six – I cried for her.

The Indian maiden whom James Stewart wooed and won in *Broken Arrow* elicited the same feelings from the adolescent me. I know it had something to do with the iconic, unpimply perfection of them up there. The girls I took to the cinema on dates stood no chance against them. We would emerge from the escapist womb and I would see us as slightly shabby and prosaic humans with no possibility of scaling the heights of danger, romance and passion which we had just vicariously experienced. I usually preferred going to the cinema on my own.

In this way I could lust uninterruptedly after Marilyn Monroe, Veronica Lake and Vivien Leigh. These ladies were occasions of sin. On the other hand, Doris Day, Debbie Reynolds and the other girls-next-door had a strangely antiseptic effect. To lust after them would have been unimaginable. They were pretty, talented, and could sing and dance, but they were not candidates for furtive fumbling in the back seat of car or cinema.

This changed with Ginny Moorehead in *Some Came Running*. Here was Shirley MacLaine with legs up to her neck, talent and sex oozing out of her, but with an innocence that harked back to my Indian-maiden period. I realised that you could have it both ways.

The next logical step was to become worthy of such wonderful women. I aspired to be casual, sophisticated, tough but kind, good-looking, strong, manly and able to sing like Frank Sinatra. All I really learned was how to dangle a fag from the corner of my mouth like Humphrey Bogart. Having done all this, it was disturbing to find that women didn't throw themselves at me. I decided the intellectual approach was better – and cheaper.

But a date was not a date if you didn't go to the pictures.

For one such rendezvous I arranged to meet the girl outside the Stella Cinema in Rathmines, on the brilliant presumption that I could persuade her to go for a walk instead. As a precaution I borrowed a half-crown from my mother ('only until tomorrow, Ma') and cycled the three miles to the cinema. But my date was wearing wobbly high heels and it was raining. I had to spend the entire budget on one-and-threepenny seats. I remember nothing about the film because I spent the whole time worrying about how in the name of ~~Jesus~~ I was going to get her home. I couldn't give her her bus fare, I couldn't even buy her an interval ice-cream or a coffee afterwards.

Fortunately the rain had stopped. I collected my bike and indicated the crossbar. Her raised eyebrows said: 'In this clean dress? What kind of eejit do you think I am?' So we walked. All the way to Inchicore. The intellectual discussion lasted five minutes. The rest was grim silence.

The other great movie disaster I had was when I got my first job. A man in the office wanted to wean his lovely niece away from the ne'er-do-well she was going out with. He offered me the money to take her out to the pictures, assuming that my charm would do the rest. He would meet me on O'Connell Bridge at 7:30 to give me the money. The girl would be at the Metropole at 8:00. Of course he didn't turn up, and in those lean days nobody had spare cash for such emergencies. I had to meet the girl and, completely humiliated, explain the whole thing to her.

In a Hollywood film I should have ended up twenty-five years later married to one of those girls. But I never saw either of them again. That's the difference between life and the movies. Give me the movies every time.

Clare McKeon

A school mystery tour. After the Zoo and Kilmainham Jail we found ourselves on the school coach in front of the Savoy Cinema on O'Connell Street.

The nuns lined us up on the footpath and we filed in. Six or seven years old, I had never seen the inside of a cinema before. Once past the usherette I raced down into the auditorium. I saw all the seats and realised I had to sit in the front in the middle, or else, I felt, I wouldn't see a thing.

Having found the desired seat, I climbed up onto it and excitedly waited for the show to start. I was entranced by the whole affair. The big screen, the colour, the glamour and excitement were intoxicating. After the programme ended the main feature started. It was *Doctor Dolittle*. It was a wonderful film and Rex Harrison was 'the business'.

As Rex was halfway through 'Talk to the animals', disaster struck. The seat I was sitting on suddenly seemed to give way under me and I crashed ungracefully to the floor – much to the delight of my classmates, who screamed with laughter.

I climbed back into my seat and went on with the film, but my concentration was shot. Off I went again, scattering crisps over everyone around me. The third time I fell, Sister Ursula swept down the aisle with her gown billowing out behind her. She made a beeline towards the source of the laughter and hilarity which was obviously out of sync with the events on the screen.

What did I think I was doing! she demanded to know in a fierce whisper. I disintegrated into tears and got more upset when the usherette arrived with her torch, blinding me in the process.

But it was the usherette who saved the situation, working out why I kept falling: I was attempting to watch the film while sitting on the edge of an upturned seat – the position they normally rest in when no one is sitting on them.

Maureen Potter
Wallace Beery versus David Copperfield

Seeing Grace Moore in *One Night of Love* twelve times in a week is my strangest memory of early days at the cinema. It happened in the lovely Queen's Theatre in the days of CineVariety – a common feature of Dublin entertainment in those days – which consisted of a film followed by a variety show followed by a film and so on throughout the day. I was in the variety show in the Queen's that week, and I spent my time between shows listening to Miss Moore and her glorious voice. Don't ask me who else was in it. I'm sure Hugh Leonard could tell me.

When my enlightened mother, God bless her, heard how I had occupied time between shows she packed me off the following Monday with a book. So I spent the week with David Copperfield rather than Wallace Beery, a more suitable companion for my age group. That set the pattern for sojourns in the Theatre Royal and the Capitol, where I read many more books than I saw films.

Those days seem light-years away, but they were brought flooding back when I started rehearsals with Joe Dowling for Hugh Leonard's wonderful play *Da*. References in the script to Buck Jones, Moot Gibson, Jim McCoy and Maria Montez, and that lovely line from the Yellow Peril, 'Wouldn't Edward G. Robinson put you in mind of a monkey?' put me in mind of days in Dublin before we lost the Queen's, the Royal and the Capitol.

Ah, those were the days, my friends... but they did end, worse luck.

Agnes Bernelle

I spent the first thirteen years of my life in the city in which I was born – Berlin – and all my early recollections are therefore connected to the German cinema.

I was five years old the first time I was taken to see a film. This is so long ago that I'm not anxious to mention the number of years, but I can recollect the event most vividly. The film was *Charlie Chaplin's Circus* – at least I think that was its title. It was, after all, about the circus, and the last shot showed Chaplin being left behind on the road while the circus wagons roll along. It had a devastating effect on me to see poor Charlie vainly trying to catch up with them. I burst into tears and sobbed so desperately that my parents could not get me to leave for home for ages – and the cinema staff had to wait for me to calm down before they could let in the customers for the next showing. My parents were reluctant to bring me to the cinema thereafter, but fortunately for me they didn't have to. There was a perfectly good small cinema right across the square on which we lived, and as soon as I was allowed to cross the road on my own, I was able to take myself to see as many films as possible. I must have watched hundreds of films, as I knew every actor and actress in the German film industry by name. I was also helped in this by the brief illustrated publication UFA Films used to deliver to people's doors every week. It was always a mixture of still photographs from one of their newest films, with a synopsis of the plot and a cast list. When my own father began to write and direct films, this knowledge stood me in good stead, as I became his unofficial casting director – I knew many more film stars' names and types than he did. I wonder how many German stars had an inkling that they owed their leading roles in my father's films to a nine-year-old girl!

When I was seven, a colleague of my father's, the film director Joe May, needed a little boy for a film he was making for UFA. Unable to find what he wanted amongst the male children he interviewed, he asked me to play 'little Peter'. I was dressed in a blue sailor suit with a matching cap, but nobody dared cut off my hair as Joe was quite keen on the then-fashionable short fringe I wore. I had my scene with one of the leading German character actors of the day, Jacob Tiedke, and some hapless young lady (possibly a friend of one of the producers) who was cast as my nanny. Fortunately (!), she couldn't act to save her life. The scene had to be reshot with another actress, and I had another day of bliss.

A year or so later an offer came from Paramount in Paris for the little 'boy' to come over to be put under contract. He was to bring his sailor suit and his fringed 'wig' with him. I was thrilled, but the thrill turned to heartbreak when my father refused to let me go, saying that my schooling was more important – I could always go into films when my education was finished.

I often wonder if he would have stopped me then if he had been aware of the imminent coming of Adolf Hitler and the consequences of this Nazi take-over for our own family, who would be forced into exile to save our lives. And I can't help thinking that my life would have been entirely different if I had gone to France to become a child star.

Sheamus Smith

While 1940s America had the movies, we in Ballaghadereen, Co. Roscommon, went to 'the pictures'. As in *Cinema Paradiso*, the local cinema, the Roxy, was owned by the church – not that the priest needed to censor the films, given the enthusiasm with which that task was undertaken by the official film censor in Dublin.

From outside the Roxy one could see into Barrack Street, where Mr Macken, the cinema manager, lived. Every weekend myself and my pals, Michael Murphy and Paddy Regan, would arrive at the cinema long before opening time. From there we monitored Mr Macken's progress as he left his home carrying a small leather attaché case containing the rolls of entrance tickets.

Laurel and Hardy, and Abbott and Costello, are among my first memories of the big screen, along with Hopalong Cassidy, that most elegant of all cowboys with his black outfit and splendid white horse, Silver. We three wanted to emulate the popular cowboys, so whilst awaiting a time when we could leave home and move to the Wild West, we contented ourselves with riding the range in a nearby field and fighting our gun battles in the town's quiet streets.

How Green Was My Valley is the first dramatic film I remember (I was fortunate enough to meet its director, John Ford, in later life). This was also the first film I saw twice, the second time in the company of my parents, sitting in the balcony, the preserve of adults. Much to my parents' embarrassment, I sought to tell them and everyone else in the balcony what was about to happen.

On regular trips to Dublin by train, my mother, indulging my great love for the cinema, took me to the Savoy and the Carlton, on more than one occasion coming out of a show in one cinema and walking straight across O'Connell Street to another complete show in the other. The trips stopped in 1949 when the whole family moved to Dublin, settling in Glenageary. Thereafter my school days were filled not with academic distinction but with the anticipation and reality of going to the pictures at the old Astoria – happily still with us as the Forum in Glasthule – the

Adelphi in Dun Laoghaire (of which I attended both the opening and the closing) and the Pavilion. Many filmic memories remain from those days – *Wuthering Heights, Gone with the Wind, Johnny Belinda*... Much later I saw Lewis Gilbert's *Sink The Bismarck*, starring my now close friend Dana Wynter, whom I subsequently saw alongside James Cagney in *Shake Hands With The Devil*. During a long but singularly one-sided love affair with the movie star Ann Blyth, I visited every suburban cinema in Dublin on my bicycle, sometimes seeing one of her films as many as seven or eight times. The affair cooled somewhat when I subsequently met the lady at a party in Hollywood many years later!

THE PLAYBOYS OF THE WESTERN

Pat McCabe

I'm afraid the first time I was in a cinema wasn't very exciting. As a matter of fact it wasn't even a cinema, just a hall where they played snooker and sometimes bingo. But on this particular occasion they had decided to show some movies. I can't recall exactly why. I think it had something to do with TB or something, because it was for a good cause and we were all allowed to go. So off we went, armed to the teeth with Taytos, lucky lumps and cough-no-mores, for the time of our lives. It was exciting going in there – everything dark, sugar paper pinned to the windows and people saying 'Not long now till the big film!' But in the immortal words of the bard, as it turned out, 'No squib was e'er damper than what met our eyes thon day'.

Not that it was all bad. It started off very promisingly with a cartoon of Daffy Duck bemoaning his outcast state as usual. Proceedings then dipped a little as on came one of these dentist films with talking germs going round the place like tail-less tadpoles giving you advice about how to take care of your teeth. Then there were a few ads with the famous CG&P shell opening and closing and this fellow who talked like no one I ever met saying 'Vera Brady's for Bridal wear' and 'McDowell's – the Happy Ring House!'

When at last the big picture came on, it was a disaster no matter what way you looked at it. Roy Rogers was in it, but whatever he was at he had no horse. He was driving around in a Morris Minor. And that was all he seemed to do – drive around and stop every so often to lean over fences and talk to this fellow and that fellow. It was no addition at all. When in the end he drove off into the sunset, I was glad, to tell you the truth. There was a pall of gloom hanging over the whole town that night. And it was understandable: when people go to see a Western, whether it is in a hall or anywhere else, what they want are ridges full of Indians and burning wagons and mean hombres and rattlers and girls standing waving goodbye bawling their eyes out. They don't want people driving around in vans. Sure you could see that any time standing on the Newtown Road.

So I think it only fair, considering it was a bit of a flop and also took place in what was really a bingo hall, that I should be allowed special dispensation to talk about the first time I saw a film in a cinema. It was *El Cid* and such an amount of slaughtering and yowling I had never seen before in my life. Because Charlton Heston was fighting for us (the Christians), the nuns made sure we all went to it. I have to say that I didn't like it because I got fed up with Charlton throwing back his cloak and staring off at nothing every five minutes. But the fight scenes were good.

I started going to the cinema regularly after that, except of course if you called it that no one would know what you were talking about. In fact you might find that you were running the risk of getting a hiding by calling it that. Some boys might say to you 'What are you talking about? It's a picture house, not a cinema. You'd do well to watch yourself.' Whatever it was, there were some pictures in that house. I think my favourite of all time was *Kiss the Girls and Make Them Die*. It was about secret agents, and such an amount of women I never seen before in my life. I saw a couple of good art ones too. There was one called *Four in the Morning* in black and white. Nothing happened in it except some girl throwing herself off a bridge and everyone looking like all belonging to them had been wiped out in a nuclear disaster. But it definitely contributed to some kind of spiritual awakening, and I walked around in a trance for a few weeks afterwards. When my mother said 'Will you go up the town and get a quarter of corned beef?' I just looked at her with sad dead eyes and although my lips moved no sound came out. There were the other ones too, with shooting and walkabout-Daleks, trees that ate people on islands, lads saying 'I laff you' to beautiful blonde girls. You name it. And then of course Clint came along and told the cowboys that they would have to apologise to his mule or else. After that I was never the same, and any time there's a fly around I keep hoping he'll land on my face and take a bit of a stroll around it for a while. Then I can go 'Ay heh heh' and flick my fag. Which is probably what the editor will do with this article.

But of all the films I ever saw since that first night in the cinema, I would say that *Jesse James meets Frankenstein's Daughter* was by far the best. Morris Minors – forget it!

Hugh McCabe

During the 50s in the Irish countryside, there were no televisions, telephones or indoor toilets. The only people who had cars were priests, doctors and rich farmers. Radios were only beginning to appear in most people's houses.

For the young, evenings were spent hurling in the local field and later, as Radio Luxembourg came on the air, listening to the latest pop records. Only a few homes had record players. The older members of society typically retired to the bar.

The single other passion for the old and young was the local cinema. In my village, those pictures were of enormous value. We came twice a week to learn at the knee of Tom, the projectionist, about the vast world outside our village and country. He taught us about the good and the bad beyond our borders. I cannot imagine how we could have coped with the maddening boredom of that time without the 'magic carpet' of the cinema. In an era of practically no private cars, here was an entertainment medium which broke the shackles of our imprisonment, transporting us to far-off countries and different periods of history.

The priest ran the cinema and took a slice of the action. It was no surprise that when Anew McMaster or the Carnival came to the village the priest always banned National School students from going to them. They cut into profits. Anyone caught going to these would face the wrath of the priest in school the next day. This was particularly hurtful for us young people who were out of our minds with boredom.

I was very fortunate to live in a village in County Kilkenny which, by the standards of that time, had a good cinema (a village two miles away occasionally showed pictures on Friday night, but their 'cinema' was no more than an empty turf shed with the small projector held precariously on top of a few boxes). The downstairs or ground floor had long wooden benches (no backs) and an admission price of sixpence. Upstairs were padded seats which cost one shilling and sixpence. The projectionist occupied a separate room at the back with two projectors. The movies were shown two nights each week – Thursday and Sunday. Listings for each month were printed on a long sheet of paper and then hung up in each shop and pub, not only in our village but in those within a ten-mile radius. Every time a new list appeared the word got around and we all headed off to see what was coming.

The names of the actors were scanned for our old favourites – Alan Ladd, Randolph Scott, Gregory Peck, John Wayne (his name was always greeted with cheers). We literally lived from Thursday night to Sunday night and then from Sunday night to Thursday night. Our daily conversations were sprinkled with 'There's a good picture on Thursday night; are you going?' 'Oh, yes, I can't wait to see it!' And then an occasional 'I hope Tom's OK that night!'

The night of the pictures was a great social event. We slicked our hair back with Brylcreem and headed off, hoping on the way to see what 'talent' appeared from the outlying villages. People would congregate outside the picture hall before it opened, to speak with friends who had cycled in from the outlying villages.

The entertainment started at 8:00 pm with 'shorts'. These were usually of a travelogue nature. We spent many hours looking at beautiful gardens, fountains and buildings in distant places which we'd never dream of ever getting to. We tolerated these, but only to a point. Occasionally they dragged on too long and this was communicated to Tom in the usual manner: hundreds of feet pounded and stamped the wooden floor whilst the air was rent by a cacophony of shrill ear-piercing whistles (many of the clientele were farmers who had perfected the fine art of shrill whistling to control dogs, cattle and so on). The floor was covered with sawdust – I have since often wondered if it was placed there to mute these feet-stamping sessions (which, incidentally, would have been superb sound effects for a stampeding herd on a Western movie set). After the shorts, 'trailers' of upcoming movies were shown. Then we finally arrived at the main reason for having come there.

Our projectionist, who was well matched to the standards of the 'cinema', had never graduated from any professional training school. Of course we, his clientele, were not particularly sophisticated either, and so he usually met our modest demands. Halfway through every picture, there was always a sudden clatter and bang accompanied by a few moments of pitch blackness as the film on one projector ran out and the other projector was switched in. Most nights it was over almost before we realised what was happening, and we picked up the movie to the noticeably different hum of the fully-loaded projector. Occasionally Tom didn't quite manage such a smooth transition. Sometimes it was because of problems with the projectors themselves, or because Tom had made a wrong connection and blown a fuse. If, however, Tom had been 'making merry' that day, the transition took more than a few moments. In such instances we were plunged into a pitch-black abyss.

We usually waited for about ten seconds, expecting the show to be resumed at any moment, but as the darkness dragged on, the primitive mode of communication with Tom was called forth; starting with a few boots, it escalated at the speed of light into a thunderous rumble which shook the wooden benches on which we sat. Since the floor upstairs was concrete, the more well-heeled in that region vented their frustration on us below by taking their cigarette butts and sending them in an arching trajectory down on top of us. In the total blackness of the cinema, the only thing visible was this flurry of red points of light moving towards our heads and necks. Miraculously, the sawdust on the floor never caught fire.

Another type of incident simply couldn't be blamed on a faulty projector or blown fuse, and unsophisticated as we were, we were smart enough not to be fooled! One particular instance during a Western movie sticks in my mind. A local spinster who never went to the pictures had inexplicably decided to come that night. Everything was going along fine, and the atmosphere in the saloon encounter between the two arch-enemies was growing tense, when there was a momentary blank screen followed immediately by the burial of the gunslingers. Another momentary blank screen and we witnessed the shootout in the street, followed by the scene where the two protagonists agreed to settle their differences in the street outside. By this time the jig was up; we lost all patience with Tom's drinking bouts in the hours before our eagerly-anticipated evening's entertainment. The rumble erupted with a vengeance and the flying butts traced dark lines across the movie screen. This mayhem continued until it was felt that the point had been gotten across to Tom. I particularly pitied the person two seats in front of me. The spinster was sitting behind him and when Tom started showing reels out of sequence, she became confused and began tapping him on the shoulder, asking questions about what was going on. She nearly drove this poor person to distraction.

Epilogue:
Over the years, incidents have occurred that brought me back with a thundering bang to that humble, simple cinema. Some twenty years after I left the village and Ireland, my family and I were in a motel in Texarkana, Texas, one very hot July night. Sudden there was a blinding flash of lightning outside and a vicious bang of thunder. I stuck my neck out the door to observe subtropical nature acting out a temper tantrum. Looking towards the end of the motel block, I saw sheets of water shooting down on a collection of palm trees which were bent over backwards in the hurricane winds. For a split second the years vanished

and I was back in that village cinema, watching Key Largo with its hotel windows being shattered and the palm trees outside being bent over by a tropical hurricane. 'By God, Tom, you were correct about that one; that's exactly what happens in these hurricanes,' I shouted.

Karl McDermott

When my mother was very young and she saw the MGM lion roar in the cinema she thought to herself, 'Oh no, not another Tarzan movie'. My father had fonder memories of the Lord of the Jungle. In fact, it was at a Tarzan movie that he saw his first pair of breasts. Then again, they belonged to Johnny Weissmuller.

My earliest memories of the cinema lack the excitement my father felt. The fact that *Finian's Rainbow* was the first movie I ever saw might explain this. Three hours of Fred Astaire and Tommy Steele searching for a crock of gold whilst conversing in two of the worst Irish brogues ever heard wasn't an ideal introduction to the delights of the big screen. At least I was spared *The Sound of Music*. What makes adults think their children will enjoy musicals?

I survived the early disappointment. In fact I even started to like the cinema, but to be honest, some of the choices I made in those early years were of Finian-esque proportions. Has anyone seen a Telly Savalas movie released in 1975 called *The Diamond Mercenaries*?

My local cinema in Galway was the Town Hall. Dank seats, stale cigarette smoke, sticky floors and Fox's Glacier Mints. A fleapit's fleapit, yet a sort of adventure. Being (and looking) under twelve and having a pathological hatred of musicals, I had quite a a limited choice on offer. I'd watch anything I was allowed to see, hence the aforementioned Telly Savalas blunder. Other errors of judgement from those years included endless dodgy film spin-offs from endless dodgy British sitcoms, a couple of dubbed movies that looked great on the posters, and a movie called *S.W.A.L.K.*, with Mark Lester and Jack Wild, which was a real disaster because not only did no one get killed, but nobody even started a fight.

But all was forgiven whenever the next Bruce Lee or James Bond movie opened. It seems hard to believe nowadays, but *From Russia With Love* was playing in Galway as late as 1974. Stranger still, it was rated an over-15s film. One wet Sunday afternoon in November, eight people stood in the queue to see that early Bond adventure. Only seven people got in to see the movie, though. The sad unfortunate who didn't was forced to ring home, get collected and watch the Sunday matinée RTE had lined up – *Tarzan the Ape Man*.

Brendan Kennelly
The Egg Store Man

The pictures in Ballylongford were held in Walsh's Egg Store, a long building at the edge of the village. The word 'film' was unknown; it was always 'the pictures', and they were 'put on' every Monday night. The favourites were Westerns starring, preferably, John Wayne. Gene Autry was acceptable but he sang too much, and he lacked the heroic dourness of John Wayne. Hopalong Cassidy wasn't bad either, largely because of the presence of his bearded, muttering old cohort, Gabby Hayes, who was, it was rumoured, a distant cousin of the Hayeses from Tarbert. But nobody could touch John Wayne.

John used to get into a lot of trouble with Indians. There was a passionate Egg Store man by the name of Stevie Moroney who took a personal interest in John Wayne's safety. At that moment in all early films when the Apaches were creeping up behind our hero, Stevie Moroney would rise from his seat, run down the middle of the Egg Store, stop in front of the screen and shout:

'John! John! Look out! Look out! Them bloody Indians are behind you!'

This warning always worked. John Wayne inevitably appeared to heed the warning, and looked behind him in time to knock off that sly, creeping, would-be Apache assassin.

The minute the lights went on after the picture, the people stayed sitting down, discussing the whole thing.

That Egg Store hatched a few rare ideas about the nature of the Western. And to be honest, I'm still an ardent John Wayne fan.

THE BOYS (AND GIRLS) IN THE BACKROOM

Gay Byrne

I grew up in the South Circular Road area, where there were two cinemas, the Rialto and the Leinster. I remember queuing in the 'four-penny rushes' on Saturday and Sunday afternoons to see films with Hopalong Cassidy and Roy Rogers.

The trouble with the fourpenny rushes and the ninepenny rushes was that you weren't guaranteed a seat; added to this uncertainty was the danger that if you misbehaved, it wasn't unusual for the ushers to take off their belts and beat the crowds of queuing children – this practice was very common in tough areas like Fairview, where mad kids were regularly whacked by angry ushers.

I remember it was very posh to go to the Carlton or the Savoy in O'Connell Street. For three and ninepence or seven shillings you were able to book ahead for Sunday night shows and had the luxury of knowing that you were assured a seat – this was a great comfort!

Round about the time I was growing up, and for some years before, it was actually possible to barter your way into the pictures with jam jars – for four or five of these items you gained entrance, and the cinema claimed the returns.

I had the good fortune of having an older brother who was a projectionist with a cinema in Inchicore; he was able to bring his kid brother and that kid brother's pals in for free to Saturday and Sunday afternoon shows. This practice continued when he moved on to the Regal in Hawkins Street and then the Queen's Theatre in Pearse Street. In the Queen's they had 'CineVariety', which took the form of an hour-long stage show of comedians and musicians with an hour of film to follow. This was the highlight of my week – and indeed I was an unusual and lucky child in that I went to the pictures every week and was regularly in projection boxes.

When I left school at eighteen I became assistant manager in the Fairview and Strand cinemas. I was based mainly in the Strand, which I remember had a bowling alley. This 1,500-seater did particularly well with *Roman Holiday*; we had the first run after the city cinemas and played to packed houses for two solid weeks. The cinema emptied and filled three times a day, breaking all records not only for ticket sales but for ice cream sales as well. When *Roman Holiday* was shown on television recently it brought back vivid memories of sitting in the manager's office and listening to the soundtrack over and over again.

Kathleen Quinn

Dublin in the 30s was very swinging – there was always a big crowd of people going to cinemas and restaurants. I was working as a maid in the United Services Club on St Stephen's Green when the manageress there, a Miss Brady, left to become a manageress in the Adelphi on Abbey Street, which was opening as a cinema and restaurant. So I went with her to the Adelphi. The Adelphi was very posh, with a circular restaurant on the first floor that looked down into the foyer. You'd go up the steps and the restaurant was built round the whole floor upstairs. But I didn't like the Adelphi much, so I left and went to the Capitol on Prince's Street, where I didn't stay for very long either. Finally, about 1937, I went to the Savoy on O'Connell Street, where I spent the next three or four years.

The Savoy was the grandest cinema in Dublin, with a wonderful restaurant. It was *the* place to eat. I worked there as a vegetable maid, one of two. We had several kitchens. The head chef – Gygax was his name – was Swiss, a smashing man and a great cook. Below him was another chef, Michael Germain from Dublin, who did all the sweets. Then there were two kitchen porters, washing the pots. They even had two men whose only job was to do the silver. It was a good union house, the Savoy. We got union rates and union hours because the manager, Mr Markey, allowed the union to keep a closed shop there.

(In the last year I was at the Savoy they had one other cook, a confectioner who had her own kitchen upstairs. She did sponges and cakes for the shop – the Savoy had a shop next door. That shop... You'd think nowadays that they invented take-away, but they had it in the Savoy in the 1940s. They had little wax cartons and they did chicken in aspic and that sort of thing. So if somebody wanted a meal to take home with them, they just went into the shop and got it.)

In the morning when we went in, we'd have breakfast: if the second chef (Gerry Ferns, an Englishman who'd come over for the Eucharistic Congress in 1932 and stayed) was in before us, he'd have a tray of bacon or something cooked. (We got all our food in the Savoy – we had a huge staff room upstairs.) Then Gerry and the kitchen porter (I forget his name, but he was a Dublin man) would have a big argument about the war, about how the Germans were doing and how the British were doing, and this would all be drafted on the table, on the chopping block with knives. 'Oh, we're doing fine.' 'No, you're not doing fine.' (One day, the kitchen porter disappeared. He'd given the impression that he couldn't stand England, but when he didn't turn up for work two days running, we found out that he'd gone over to England and joined the army. Gerry Ferns'll never forget it.) We went in at about 9:00 or 9:30 in the morning and prepared for the day.

The restaurant opened about 11:30. Lunch was on between 12 and 2, and then some of the staff would have hours off. Maybe you'd have three hours off, until six, and then you'd be there till 12 – a split shift. All the staff had free passes to the cinema, and we always used them. So during your free time you'd probably go to the cinema.

It wasn't a given that if you were going to the Savoy restaurant you'd go to the cinema. Businessmen would come in, and people 'up from the country'. They had this orchestra of about six women – Madame Ballalas and her ladies – and they came in at lunch-time and played all the topical music, on the bandstand in the middle of the floor. It was a very grand place.

I was there when I got married in 1940. I left the Savoy in 1942.

They were hard-working times, but it was a good life as well. Your expectations of all these pleasures weren't so high; and besides, we had our cinema and there was quite a lot of life going on. The Savoy was like a home in a way, we spent so much time there.

Chalmers (Terry) Trench

'I'm not a regular film-goer. I only go once a week,' said a female clerk in my office in Drogheda, some time in the 1940s or 50s. At that time there were two cinemas in Drogheda, changing their programmes twice weekly, so that you could, if you chose, see a different show six nights a week. Of necessity, these cinemas competed with each other for the films having the widest popular appeal – nothing 'arty', no foreign languages. And during the 1939-1945 'Emergency', the standard of what was available was pretty low.

I was a late-comer to the cinema (I was sixteen before I saw my first film, a Charlie Chaplin picture, in the south of France); but I was friendly with Eddie Toner, one of the founder members of the Irish Film Society, and was a regular attender at their showings in the Classic in Terenure during the short time I lived in Terenure, between 1940 and 1942, before moving to Drogheda.

It happened one day that a lay teacher in the Christian Brothers' School – Peadar McCann, perhaps the most intellectually interesting man in Drogheda – stopped me in the street and asked whether we could start a Film Society there. In July 1945, we had a meeting in the Drogheda Chamber of Commerce room in the Whitworth Hall, at which Alderman Dennis, then Mayor of Drogheda, spoke of the 'excellent aims' of the Film Society: 'raising the standard of film appreciation and the creation of a demand for a better type of film.'

Our initial proposition was to project eight films during the following winter season, showing, to members only, pictures of special merit which might not have a big enough general appeal to make them a paying undertaking for cinema proprietors. To enable us to start we needed 130 members paying an annual subscription of a guinea each. By September 1945 we were approaching this figure and had booked programmes for eight 'midnight matinées' to be shown on 35 mm, one each month from October to May, in the Abbey cinema, after the cinema's regular programme.

We showed nine features and sixteen shorts from Europe, the USA and the USSR. We distributed a questionnaire to our 163 members at the end of the first season, and received thirty-seven replies, of which twenty-two expressed satisfaction with the season's programme. One member, on the other hand, singled out *Hortobagy*, a beautiful and sensitive record of life on the plains of Hungary, describing it as 'for the most part a gross insult'. We could only presume that this outburst was due to the inclusion of a scene showing a foal being born (although I don't think we saw the antecedent to the birth).

In October 1946 we started our second season, continuing to use the Abbey. In addition, however, we showed a series of programmes in St Peter's Church Hall at 8 pm, for the benefit of members who preferred this time to the 'midnight matinées' which started at 10:20 pm. Membership, however, dropped – with transport restrictions lifted (private motoring had been prohibited from April 1942 until December 1945) and with the wide variety of pictures available in Dublin, there no longer seemed to be the same need for a Drogheda branch of the Irish Film Society. Rather than see it decline further, we decided, after completion of the second season, to wind it up while it was still in a relatively healthy state.

John MacKenna
Peter Murphy... and Christmas

Did word spread as far as Athy? Probably not. Word of Peter Murphy and the Castle Cinema, Castledermot? Probably not. Didn't Athy have its own cinema in the 50s and 60s? Why should Castledermot concern the good people of this parish!

But for us, snotty-nosed brats of the late 50s and early 60s, Peter Murphy was entertainment for Castledermot. He owned and ran the cinema. Open every Wednesday, Friday and Sunday for pictures and for dances in between. The dances were of no concern to us. Dancing was 'thick'. Love and romance were 'thick'. The pictures were the real thing. And Peter Murphy was the pictures.

Never a Friday night went by that he didn't appear onstage at the interval to tell us about the coming week's attractions. He tossed off the names of films and stars, plots were rolled into one sentence, and occasionally there was the aside – 'This film stars Audie Murphy – no relation'. I'm told there were times when Peter played the violin at the interval. I never witnessed that, but I don't doubt it; it was part of the style that was his – a style we might mock, but a style we admired.

Whether we were in the 'woodeners' at the front, the halfway house inside the door or the plush seats at the back, we were impressed by the way he ran the place. And there was running in it. We mostly went to see the pictures but there were other businesses that took up our time. Trying to get people in free through the side door; shouting half-baked encouragement to the courting couples in the back row; playing the piano that was parked in the hallway outside the toilets – especially during the film; trying to sneak from the cheap seats to the plusher models without being caught... It was all part of the action. Until the big picture started. Then we shut up and settled down.

But that was all mundane stuff.

Christmas in the picture-house was the real thing – especially Stephen's Day and the matinée. After a bleak period and no television – I'm talking 60s here – this was release, freedom, adventure and hope. Pockets stuffed with sweets from the tin of Roses spilled under the couch in the sitting-room, a thick slice of Christmas cake in hand for the journey to the picture-house, an imaginary horse to get me there in time and I was off.

Inside the picture-house there was a tree, decorations dancing as the door opened and closed, parcels piled underneath, lights glimmering. The place was warm and had that smell of seats and timber and pleasantly stale air, the smell of picture-houses everywhere. But there was something special about it on this one day. Because this was more than an outing to the pictures – this was as much a part of childhood Christmas as the crib or midnight Mass or Santa Claus or carol singers or the roasting smell of turkey or the boiling smell of ham. This was Christmas carried over to the day after everything was supposed to have ended; this was the season carried on, the light kept burning in the dark days after festivity. The picture-house was our refuge, Peter Murphy was our saviour. It was as plain as that. And after all the hard words of the previous year, the Sunday afternoons when our shouts were too loud and his hand tapped us on the shoulder with a warning 'gotcha'; after the occasional evening when we were escorted to the door and barred for the coming week – this was the season of peace and goodwill, even to snotty-nosed brats who were investigating the shoreline between behaving themselves and being cheeky.

Stephen's Day afternoon was Christmas all over again.

After the small picture the lights came up in the cinema and the raffle began. We all clutched our tickets, given free at the door, and one by one the numbers were pulled. My memory is that no one went away empty-handed. The packages were handed out and were opened with the same excitement that we'd felt the day before. And then the lights went down and the big picture started. There was music, colour, loud voices, adventure, happy endings. We sat glued to the screen and when the closing credits rolled we were loath to stir, until the crackly strains of the National Anthem drew us to our feet. And then the doors opened and we poured out into the late-afternoon gloom, our guns cracking as we galloped across the School Lane and dispersed to the town or the woodlands or the low terrace or the high terrace. From there on it was downhill to the new year; but we had that memory, that warm feeling that something good had happened, that we had been part of a communal event in the picture-house, that all the snide remarks and feuds that are part of children's lives were unimportant.

There were few enough people then who would put as much thought and effort into bringing us together and making that day special as Peter Murphy did. He was eccentric in the best sense of the word – his life was a Hollywood story off the screen, or at least that's how it seemed to me. He was technicolour in a monochrome time of my life; he was larger than life. Sometimes I think he was more influential in my life than I realised. He bucked the system, did his own thing, stood up and was counted in ways that were different. He was himself and he was never afraid or ashamed to be that person. All that sank into my mind, and into the minds of many others.

No doubt Athy had characters like him, but none could have been the same – none could have made the impression he made on so many of us. Partly it was because the village we lived in was so small. But it wasn't just that – it was the fact of how Peter Murphy chose to be his own man in spite of what people thought of him. The turn of the year always reminds me of him and of the influence he had on our community and on myself.

I remember him at Christmas-time particularly, and I include him in the round of visits to graves in the Castledermot cemetery.

Did his fame travel the nine miles to Athy in those more difficult days of the 50s and 60s? Maybe not. It should have. It has certainly travelled down the years with me.

I close my eyes and it's Stephen's Day again and the decorations are swaying on the Christmas tree in the Castle Cinema and Peter Murphy is standing on the stage and I'm there among the eager-faced kids in the wooders and he's drawing a ticket... and it might be mine. Happy Christmas, Peter, and thanks.

MELODRAMA/
THE WOMAN'S FILM

Mary Cummins

Watching the 1996 Oscars ceremony recalled for me the Sunday after-noon matinées at the cinema in Ballybunion – the only times we were allowed to go except in the holidays. There were two lots of seats – the fourpennies under the screen or the shillingies. We could sometimes smoke with our heads down if there was enough of a crowd. Those in the courting corner at the back could do a bit more.

Mostly we got an unending diet of Westerns with not one woman in them. Once, *Mise Éire* came. And we got to see Judy Garland in *A Star is Born* because they thought it was a religious film! Very often the 'small' picture was best: a short, daft comedy with the Movietone News thrown in. As the credits rolled for the big picture my heart would drop at the unending list of men's names. It just meant wars, guns, good cowboys, bad Indians and generally, men beating the lard out of each other.

If there was a woman it meant a bit of fashion – even if it was just a long dress and a bonnet. A woman meant a bit of passion and romance. A woman meant those panic scenes when she would go into labour and everyone would run around shouting for boiling water. Then there would be silence until you heard the baby's cry...

Nell McCafferty
From Rags to the Rialto

The man arrived at two o'clock in the afternoon to take my dog away. The whole street came out to watch. There was no pretence about it. Rags was paralysed, his kidneys gone. I knew he was being taken away to the gas chamber, there to die. Why my parents allowed me to sit on the doorstep, sobbing, watching the man take Rags away to his early doom, I do not know. I was glad even then, and I am especially glad now in retrospect, that they let me keep vigil over his last hour on earth. It gives me a sane, calm perspective on TV violence today – children know what's going on. I was well able for it, though of tender years; about nine, I think. Afterwards, my mother insisted that I go to the pictures as a treat. I knew she was buying me off, wanted my misery out of her sight; I protested nobly that nothing would console me; and I went off anyway, making a sacrifice for mammy's sake, in the sickening, pious way that children do.

My Aunt Nellie received me with full honours at the Rialto cinema. Years later I realised she was secretary to the manager, not the manageress. She gave me popcorn, ice cream, a bag of sweets and my choice of seating, all free of charge. I cried a little, ate a lot – oh, Rags, what can I say? Life must go on – and was soon lost in the wonderful world of *The Wizard of Oz*. By the time I emerged, the day still young, my dog was well and truly dead and gone and buried. I sang songs from the movie all the way home. It was a great wake.

Doireann Ní Bhriain

I started to go to the cinema before television came to Ireland. When I bring my children to a film now, they're just seeing a larger version of an imagery they're already quite familiar and comfortable with. For me as a small child in the 1950s, the cinema was pure magic.

I think I was about four when I was brought to see my first film. I screamed in terror when the wicked witch in *Snow White and the Seven Dwarfs* tried to climb down off the screen to gobble me up. But that didn't stop me wanting to go back again and again into the dark cave which let me into somebody else's world for a magical few hours.

I grew up on the seafront in Baldoyle, about ten miles from the centre of Dublin. The Snow White experience took place, I think, in the Metropole and must have been around Christmas time, for that and school holidays were the only occasions on which I remember going to town during my early years.

My concrete cinema memories all have to do with our local picture house at Sutton Cross, ten minutes' walk from our house. This was not an elaborate establishment. It had a lot of the grubbiness of its counterparts in villages and towns all over the country, but its cold, tiled entrance hall and echoing toilets didn't stop it being an escapist paradise which my friends and I frequented regularly during the early 60s.

I was a discriminating cinema-goer only to the extent of refusing to go to Westerns or horror films – which left mainly the schmaltzy weepies and harmless comedies. I did not want to be frightened at the cinema and I hated films that didn't have enough women in them. So I ended up seeing some pretty awful movies; but I didn't know then that they were awful, and I felt more warm romantic glows, not to mention sexual excitement, coming out of that dungeon than I ever got across the road at the tennis club dances where the real thing was supposed to happen.

I fell in love regularly with saccharine smoothies like Richard Chamberlain, andbecame the blonde and beautiful girlfriend of Bobby Darin. And I decided, finally, to become a film actress. This was on the cards already because I had an uncle who was quite a well-known film actor in his day, and I had the feeling I could easily follow in his footsteps.

But then along came Hayley Mills and the die was cast. The main thing was that she was the same age as I was, and I suffered from a severe need to identify totally with screen heroines. Her being blonde and tall and coming from a family of successful film actors didn't deter me in the slightest. To this day, I'm not sure what the attraction was, but I saw every single film she made many times over. I knew all her lines and I progressed from being a young black-and-white twelve-year-old in Whistle Down the Wind to a sophisticated, suntanned young woman falling chastely in love with her co-star, Peter McEnery – or was it Ian McShane? That one was set on a Greek island and had a lot of windmills in it, but I can't remember what it was called. As a young teenager, I identified so closely with everything Hayley Mills did that when she turned up on a chat show on television a few years ago, I felt I'd just been reunited with a long-lost sister. Her career as an adult star never did quite take off, however, and my own never even started.

The other thing I loved at that age was musicals. I've no idea how often I went back to *Seven Brides for Seven Brothers*, *Annie Get Your Gun* or *Oklahoma*, but I do remember the sheer joy of bouncing out into rainy nights with those songs ringing in my ears. And the absolute thrill of seeing the likes of Elvis Presley, Cliff Richard and the Beatles in the flesh, as it were, on the big screen. Those were simple times.

As a young film-goer, I had no critical acumen whatever. The only contribution my formal education made to my awareness of cinema was to make me and my classmates sit through crackling prints of *The Song of Bernadette* and the like in order to further our spiritual development.

Somehow or other, I fumbled my way towards a deeper and a wider appreciation of films as I grew older. That pleasure of sliding through the darkness into someone else's world conquered my fear of celluloid witches and turned me into the inveterate cinema-goer I now am.

My hope for my own children is that Film Studies will be on their school curriculum. I'd like them to have the discrimination and the critical tools I didn't have, as well as the joy and the magic.

THE SONG REMAINS THE SAME

Eamonn Sweeney
The Birth of Cool

From an early age I have been enthralled by the craftsmen of the silver screen – those *auteurs* who have made cinema into an art form worthy of the type of attention normally received by classical music and the plays of Shakespeare. I can still remember how impressed I was by the pantheistic vision of Alexander Dovzhenko, Akira Kurosawa's extension of the conventions of Noh theatre to the movies and Ingmar Bergman's sombre Scandinavian disquisitions on life and death.

None of the above is true.

What I remember is *Quadrophenia* in the Gaiety cinema in Sligo. I am thirteen and the screen is filled with the music of The Who and interminable brilliantly-choreographed fight scenes on the Brighton beachfront. Phil Daniels is in love with his motorbike, his gang and a blonde girl played by Leslie Ash. In that order. The film hits all the right buttons for a teenager from a village of two hundred people dreaming of somewhere else. It has music, sex and violence, the essential components of the world of a teenage boy.

Quadrophenia does it for me. Above all else, what it has is cool. Everyone in that cinema is searching for cool because they know it exists even if they do not know exactly where it is. For me at thirteen, *Quadrophenia* is cool. Even that terminally naff bastard Sting manages to be cool.

Quadrophenia made me want to be a Mod. Mod was a long, green parka bought from an army surplus shop beside a river, V-necked sweaters, a bomber jacket, drainpipe jeans, winkle-picker shoes, button badges of The Jam and The Who. All graffiti had to have arrows attached to the letters. White socks must be worn. They too had their day.

I lived in Gurteen, twenty-three miles from the cinemas in Sligo town. There was a cinema in Boyle just ten miles away. But Sligo was town. Sligo was the county town. Sligo was where we went when we wanted to see Sligo Rovers win, and came home from when we'd seen them lose.

'They're a Cup team. The League doesn't suit them.'

The Gaiety and the Savoy were Sligo's two cinemas. The Gaiety is still there. The Savoy came off badly when a laundrette next door blew up. It is no more.

The Gaiety featured special double-seats, for snogging purposes – a big attraction at the time.

A meditation on the double seat:

What do you do when you bring someone to the cinema for the first time and there is the option of the double seat?

1. Take the double seat. These things are difficult enough without having to scramble across an arm-rest to get your mildly evil way. But will it look like you're expecting too much? It could put you under pressure to dive immediately into action.

2. Don't take the double seat. This puts the two of you at your ease for a while. But then. The arm-rest is there and it poses an almost insurmountable obstacle. Perhaps the girl is used to double seats and will consider two singles the height of wimpishness.

Decision time.

It's not easy being a teenager, so it's not.

I wish I remembered more abut my first experiences of the cinema. I seem to recall seeing cartoon films. The words 'Alakazam the Great' ring a bell. But my main memory of cinema as a kid is that these cartoons were always preceded by wildlife films which featured shots of a scorpion in the desert.

There's a lot said about how the cinema's glory years were the 30s and 40s. The late 70s and the early 80s are decried as some cinematic wasteland where 'the flicks' had completely lost their glamour.

None of the above is true.

Can I go back to Sligo Rovers again? Right. A match at Stamford Bridge doesn't necessarily provide you with a more intense experience than one at the Showgrounds. The crowd is ten times bigger, but the match is just as exciting for the people following Rovers. Cinema circa 1981 was the same. The gang who had stuck with the cinema still thought of it as a wonderland. We believed in the stars. We talked about what we'd seen on screen as if it was true. The more lunatic fringe of us thumbed twenty-three miles down to the cinema, and walked a lot of the distance back, to see *Mad Max* or *First Blood*. Dedication.

The Savoy inspired more affection than the Gaiety. The Savoy was the Showgrounds. The facilities were crap, the place was falling to bits, and somehow this seemed like a good thing. If you couldn't put up with a bit of discomfort, what were you doing at the pictures? The Multiplex was a long way off.

Cinema affected your everyday life in South Sligo. You'd thumb to some damp half-lit hall in the arse-end of nowhere for a disco and inevitably someone would raise a row. The next thing, the air would be full of young lads in denim jackets doing those flying kicks where you pushed off with one foot and lashed with the other. You rarely saw one connecting but almost everyone tried them. It might have been because of the long tradition of Oriental fighting arts in Ballymote, Geevagh and Ballintogher. Or it could have been the effect of watching Bruce Lee. He was cool for a while too.

When *Rocky III* came out, what was pronounced in Geevagh as 'kaawng fo' suffered a loss of popularity. Everyone I knew joined a boxing club and went back to the same halls to slug it out with the same people in tiny rings. The home fighter always got the decision. Heads hummed 'The Eye of the Tiger' to give themselves courage as they sat on their stools waiting for the third round.

I thumbed all over the country with my brother Eoghan. He was a year younger than me. That weird mixture of sentimentality and rivalry that afflicts brothers followed us round the by-roads. We both thought we were cool.

Film then was a teenage thing. It seemed almost impossible that adults would set foot in a cinema. A trendy, crimplened religion teacher recommended *The Breakfast Club* to us to show us just how trendy he was. People who normally avoided the cinemas went to see it and came home improved by its wholesome message.

We preferred *Scarface*. Violence in cool clothes, Al Pacino and the teenager's bushido code of honour. 'Tony Montano came into this world with only two things – balls of steel and my word – and I don't break either for anyone.'

We didn't want understanding and sympathy for the difficulties of being a youngster. We wanted giant automatic weapons, cocaine, dollar bills and Michelle Pfeiffer beside a swimming pool.

It was a strange time. *War Games* might have been a corny film but it captured something a lot of us felt. Your life didn't seem real sometimes. We scrawled CND signs on every available wooden surface like they were lucky charms that would ward off evil. It was the time of Chernobyl, the bombing of Libya, *Star Wars*, *Seven Minutes to Midnight*. Prince in *Sign o' the Times*.

'If night comes and the bomb falls, will you see the dawn?'

Still in search of cool. We find it in 1985. *Stop Making Sense*. Talking Heads. Directed by Jonathan Demme. David Byrne looking amazing in these impossibly baggy suits. Baggy suits were the new cool.

Into town to buy baggy suits. Deadly ones with a blue and grey fleck. The next night we hit an open-air disco in a hotel car-park. The man in the boutique had sold exactly the same suit to all of us. Eight identical suits stood in a circle on the concrete and tried to look nonchalant. Then we decided it was OK. We looked like a gang. It was enough for us.

The man who sold us the suits emigrated to Australia the year after. I went to London – the London of films like *Quadrophenia, Absolute Beginners* and *The Long Good Friday*. I left Sligo Rovers behind and went to the Bridge on Saturdays to watch Chelsea. The League didn't seem to suit them either.

Pat O'Mahony

As a nipper I can still remember being regularly packed off to the now-defunct Tower Cinema in Kildare town – named, one presumes, after the local round tower. (Later, before its eventual demise in the mid-80s, it underwent the ignominy of an overhaul that not only severely reduced its seating capacity, but also forced on it the innocuous and meaningless 'Studio One' as a new moniker). These trips were usually Sunday afternoon affairs for whatever matinée was on. We always chose the less comfortable but cheaper seats near the front, so leaving more to spend on edible delights. The thing is, while I know that many of these films were war movies and have vague recollections of the odd comedy and thriller, I'd be hard pressed to actually name more than a handful. For some reason, *The Night of the Living Dead* and *Soldier Blue*, both of which I was probably too young to see at the time, spring to mind; but the rest are a blur. I do recall being thrown out on one occasion for some sort of rowdy behaviour, though at the time I was sure it wasn't my fault.

Later, in my teens, going to the pictures in Kildare was largely a dating activity and because the big screen activity was hardly a priority, it rarely mattered what was on. I do, however, remember making a point of, on their respective releases, going to see both Led Zeppelin's concert movie *The Song Remains the Same* and The Who-inspired *Quadrophenia* – not a great shock considering my other great love in life, music.

My appetite for good cinema became almost insatiable relatively late in life. It's easy to spot the turning point: at the grand old age of twnty-two I went back to college to study communications at NIHE in

'The Palace of Delights', the Savoy, 1955

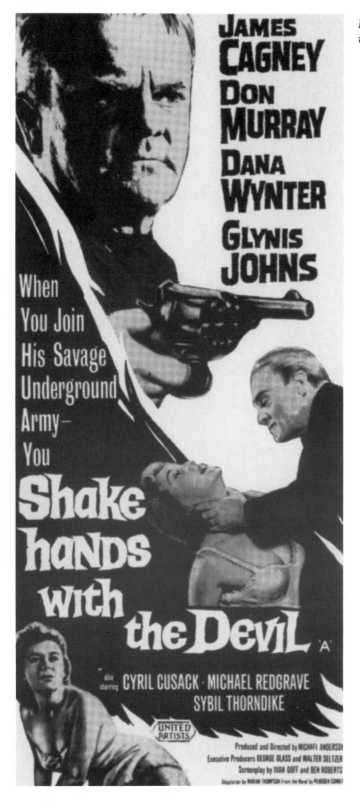

Left: Press Book *Shake Hands with the Devil*, 1959

Above: James Cagney backstage with The Royalettes, Theatre Royal, Dublin, 1958

*Below:*The Savoy Cinema and Restaurant, O Connell Street, Dublin, 1952

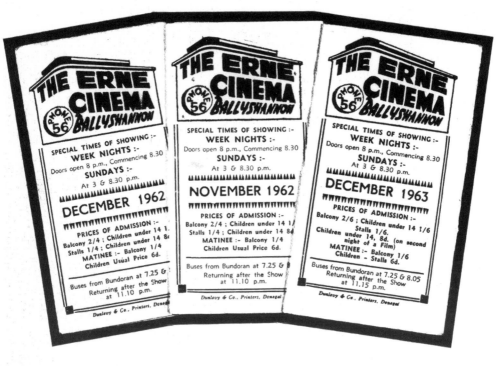

Above & below: Selection of programmes from the Erne Cinema,
Ballyshannon, County Donegal

Sunday 1st July. 3 & 8.30 p.m. 1 Day Glen Ford, Gloria Grahame in **THE BIG HEAT** Also Randolph Scott, Angela Lansbury in **LAWLESS STREET**	**Monday 9th., Tuesday 10th.** 2 Days Jennifer Jones, Gregory Peck, Joseph Cotten **DUEL IN THE SUN** (In Color). Children under 16 years cannot be admitted	**Friday 20th., Saturday 21st.** 2 Days Jean Arless, Glenn Corbett in **HOMICIDAL** Also John Crawford in **IMPERSONATOR**
Monday 2nd., Tuesday 3rd. 2 Days James Robertson Justice, Leslie Phillips in **RAISING THE WIND** In Color. Also Bernard Lee in **CLUE OF THE SILVER KEY**	**Wednesday 11th., Thursday 12th.** 2 Days Max Bygraves, Donald Pleasence in **SPARE THE ROD** Also Peter Reynolds in **QUESTION OF SUSPENSE**	**Sunday 22nd.** 3 & 8.30 p.m. 1 Day Dorothy McGuire, Ethel Barrymore in **SPIRAL STAIRCASE** Edgar Wallace Thriller **X-ROADS TO CRIME**
Wednesday 4th. 1 Day Bruce Cabot, Patricia Medina in **THE RED CLOAK** Also Dennis O'Keefe in **CHICAGO SYNDICATE**	**Friday 13th., Saturday 14th.** 2 Days Ian Carmichael, Janette Scott, Sidney James **DOUBLE BUNK** Also Donald Pleasence in **WIND OF CHANGE**	**Monday 23rd, Tuesday 24th, Wednesday 25th,** **Thursday 26th, Friday 27th, Saturday 28th.** FOR SIX DAYS **Commencing at 8 p.m. Nightly** Mitzi Gaynor, Rosanna Brazzi in Rogers and Hammerstein's
Thursday 5th., Friday 6th., Saturday 7th. (3 Days) Ponga and Perdita in Walt Disney's **lOl DALMATIANS** (In Color).	**Sunday 15th.** 3 & 8.30 p.m. 1 Day Robert Wagner, Terry Moore in **BENEATH THE 12 MILE REEF** (In Cinemascope and Color). Also Debra Paget in **GUN IN HIS HAND**	**SOUTH PACIFIC** (In Cinemascope and Color). Prices of Admission 4/6, 3/6, Child 2/4, 1/4
Sunday 8th. 3 & 8.30 p.m. 1 Day James Mason, Robert Wagner, Janet Leigh in **PRINCE VALIANT** (In Cinemascope and Color). Also Gary Merrill in **YACHT ON THE HIGH SEAS**	**Monday 16th., Tuesday 17th., Wednesday 18th.** (3 Days) Glenn Ford, Bette Davis in **POCKETFUL OF MIRACLES** (In Panavision and Color).	**Sunday 29th.** 3 & 8.30 p.m. 1 Day Gary Cooper, Susan Hayward in **GARDEN OF EVIL** (In Cinemascope and Color). Also Ricardo Montalban in **BROKEN ARROW**
	Thursday 19th. 1 Day Elvis Presley, Debra Paget, Richard Egan in **LOVE ME TENDER**	**Monday 30th., Tuesday 31st July, Wednesday** **1st August. — — — — — 3 Days** Cliff Richard, Robert Morley, Carole Gray **THE YOUNG ONES** (In Cinemascope).

The silver screen brings the Caribbean to Athenry in 1933, County Galway

Above: Kelvin Picture
Palace, Belfast *circa*
1911

Right: Exterior, Rialto
Cinema, Derry,
during the 1930s

Above left: Interior, Theatre Royal, Dublin, 1956
Below left: Exterior,Theatre Royal, Dublin 1956

Above: The Estoria Cinema, Galway (later the Claddagh Palace)
Below: The Talkies come to the Whitworth Hall, Drogheda *circa* 1929

Glasnevin (now Dublin City University), where two things combined to kick-start an interest that hasn't waned since.

First, the Film Studies section of the Communications course began to show us ways of looking at the humble flick that, prior to this, hadn't occurred to me: everything from editing tricks to the treatment of ethnic stereotypes, the meaning behind various camera angles, questions of film as a reflection of various ideologies, and the overall importance of the director over actors.

Second, I joined the college film society and for the first time in my life deliberately began to see at least one movie a week. And though the small lecture theatre with its single 16mm projector was no luxury, Dolby Surround Sound, cinematic experience, hey, who cared? This was the biz.

I'm now in the enviable position of occasionally being invited to press screenings of new movies just prior to release, though I don't get the chance to attend often enough. I still, though, regularly head out to the cinema as a paying customer, be it to one of the larger ones for a Hollywood blockbuster or to somewhere like the IFC, the Lighthouse or the Screen for something a little more offbeat. I'd like to go more, but there just don't seem to be enough hours in the day or days in the week to do everything. And just to make matters that little bit worse, I'll watch any half-decent movie that crops up on TV, even if I've seen it before, and I'll try and tape those I miss; no wonder that at any given time I've at least twenty-five or thirty VHSs waiting to be viewed.

So, after a slow start, I LOVE MOVIES. Be they old or new, comedy or horror, foreign or Irish, big-budget or independent, black-and-white or colour, in English or subtitled... as long as they're good, count me in.

Laura Magahy

My father was a bank manager and as a result we moved around the country while I was growing up. Cork was rich in cinemas – unlike today. But I particularly remember one trip to the cinema. I was about seven at the time. We were on holiday in Tramore, staying in a hotel which was being renovated so there was constant noise of construction work and the swimming pool wasn't ready. It rained every day, and overall the holiday was disastrous.

My parents were struggling to entertain three small children. One afternoon, having been barred by the hotel management from going up and down in the lift yet again, we were given a choice: a trip to the fun-fair or to the cinema. I chose to go to the cinema, a square building with red velvet seats, and my mother and I set off in the rain. The film showing was *Double Trouble*, starring Elvis Presley. While he was stunning, I loved the clothes and the glamour even more. It was a Cinderella-type story, and the 'double trouble' referred to the twin sisters, a naughty and a nice twin. I loved the bad twin. When the good twin went off to the dance with Elvis, the bad twin sneaked up behind and cut a large part out of her dress. The film transported me out of the seemingly endless grey weather in Tramore to a party life of music, intrigue and jealousy.

But while cinema was a pleasure, its pleasure was made largely available through its rival medium, television. We used to watch Westerns on television every Sunday afternoon (still raining!); and I saw wonderful musicals with Jeanette McDonald and Nelson Eddy which we then acted out and sang. Television gave a new lease of life to those old classics in our house, and it was then that I developed a taste for Westerns and 'weepies' which still remains with me today.

Alan Gilsenan
Inventing Worlds

Cinema played a surprisingly small part in my early life. This is a source of mild embarrassment to me, because the common mythology dictates that anyone aspiring to be a great film-maker must be able to recall spending every god-forsaken moment of his childhood sneaking into a cinema to watch some great classic. I, on the other hand, can only recall sneaking in late to Haddington Road church to serve Mass.

Searching for the formative cinema experiences of my youth, my mind goes back to watching my godfather's home movies projected on the wall of a dark country drawing-room after Telefís Éireann news and rosary with all the trimmings. The scratched colour films were full of religious processions, tennis parties and meetings of the Ballymacad Fox Hunt. Even then, entering the world of these films felt like opening the door on a lost era of nobler times.

Or maybe it began further back, watching my own imaginary films projected in the recesses of my boyish mind. These were often sparked off playing with my cousins Rosemary and Karena in a Ranelagh rose garden, or during idyllic summer holidays spent on my Aunt Resa and Uncle Maurice's farm outside Mullingar while my parents went to the Galway Races – playing alone in a disused railway-carriage-cum-hen-house, or inventing worlds, with my cousin Marie, by the stream that we imagined a river.

But as a child, I cannot actually remember going to the cinema often. My father loved light opera and, apart from pantomimes with Jack Cruise and Maureen ('Keep your breath to cool your porridge') Potter, my most vivid memories are of being brought to shows like *The Desert Song*, *The Merry Widow* and *South Pacific* in Kells Town Hall in Meath. These musicals have retained their magical hold on me ever since. The films I remember were also musicals with wondrous names – *Mary Poppins*, *Chitty Chitty Bang Bang* and *The Sound of Music*. Like my theatrical experiences, they bore no relation to the world in which I lived – they inhabited a world that was both fantastical and sentimental. In retrospect, these films – like *The Wizard of Oz*, which I discovered later in life – feel almost radical in their daring, imaginative scope. Such was their power that I have no recollection of the actual cinemas in which I saw them, except for a musty smell and a lingering affection for red velvet.

As childhood gave way to teenage years, cinema got lost along the way. It seemed to hold little attraction beside the screaming demands for attention from the Undertones, the Boomtown Rats, Stiff Little Fingers and other bands with obscure, punky names that have been lost to pop history. But I do remember slinking into the Sandford Cinema (now Wong's Chinese restaurant) one hot summer afternoon. The film was a rare re-run of the cultish *Easy Rider*, and my more cine-literate friends had conjured up a feeling of illicit expectation for the event – although this may have had more to do with the fact that it was over-eighteens than with the film itself. I remember virtually nothing of its content except that as we left the cinema, the previously mundane Sandford Road seemed to have changed irrevocably and to have taken on a wild, mythical dimension which it has retained ever since. I guess I also had changed and the film, like a first romance, had left the world a more wonderful if less innocent place.

Unwittingly, John Bourke may have been responsible for my cinema education being nipped in the bud. John married one of the more glamorous of those girl-cousins who had inhabited the landscape of my childhood. He always seemed – and still seems today – a fount of common sense. I recall him saying that he thought it was a bad move to bring a date to the cinema because afterwards, when you came out onto O'Connell Street on a wet Thursday evening, she was bound to look at you and think that you didn't compare favourably with the current screen idol. This seemed like sound advice at the time and I must have taken it, because after *Easy Rider*, cinema disappeared once more from my life. Instead, rather than going to watch films in the comparative safety of the back row of a cinema, I set about trying to turn my dates into films with a romantic and, at times, melodramatic storyline. As it transpired, this was a far more perilous way to spend a Saturday night.

By the time I made my first effort at making a film I was twenty-one and I couldn't remember the last time I had been inside a cinema. The grammar of cinema was lost to me and I had to try to recreate or invent it for myself as I wrote that first script through the night. Whether that has been a help or a hindrance in trying to make films, I am still not sure. Even today, I harbour a reluctance to go to the cinema, although I love it once I'm there. I think, perhaps, that it is that strange feeling of physical passivity, a feeling that I am sacrificing my life for another, that unsettles me; or maybe it is simply the plain egotism of wanting to make films instead of watching them.

Whatever it is, I'm sure that this resistance to cinema-going is perverse and that my early years would have been wonderfully enhanced by a wider experience of cinema. Looking back, I'm certain many other films have been lost to my memory; but then memory, like cinema, is essentially selective in its combination of cherished moments, and these are some of mine.

YOU DIRTY RAT...

Ben Kiely
Soft Shoes and Harry Carey

One day, I remember, when my family were younger, I was going through the morning ritual of shaving and accompanying myself in song. Like this:

'I've told every little star
Just how sweet I think you are.
Why haven't I told you?'

And my eldest daughter overheard me and said, 'Dad, you're really with it. That's the latest!'

The song, you see, had been experiencing a revival. And I looked sadly back over all the years to the day in Millers' Picture House in Omagh town when John Boles and Virginia Bruce and Douglas Montgomery electrified us all in the movie that made that song famous. Who now, except antiquarians and septuagenarians or worse, remembers John Boles or Virginia Bruce or Douglas Montgomery?

But my first picture-show was not in Millers' but in the rival house: Donnelly's Star Kinema. It was Harry Carey in a Western called *Soft Shoes*. And I was brought there by my sister Kathleen and her friend Annie Rodgers. What age I was exactly I can't remember. But the great event certainly took place the best part of seventy years ago. Quietly enough I walked between the two ladies. But I was quiet only because I was too excited to speak. I had the oddest ideas about what was going to happen in the Picture House. I thought that people came out of a thing called 'the screen' and dashed madly around the floor.

This blessed present day I remember little of the movie. But what I do remember I can see as clearly as if it were painted there on the wall before me. I see robbers with masks and pistols in a bank, and then Harry Carey riding to the rescue at a speed that no modern jet could equal. He splashes through a pool of water that reminded me of the duck-pond out at my Aunt Kate Gormley's place in Claramore. He climbs up to the roof of a high building beside the bank. Then he jumps clean through the roof of the bank, landing lightly on his feet, both guns blazing, in the middle of the somewhat surprised robbers. That Harry Carey, I decided, was a bigger man than Fionn MacCumhail.

For a month after that I was Harry Carey. I went around bang-bang-banging at friend and foe, and wearing a pair of cowboy trousers that my sister Kathleen made for me out of a potato-sack. They were the best that wee fellows at the time could come by. Nowadays, their parents buy them fancy things in shops.

I jumped wildly off high walls and shot robbers by the hundred. Now and then I condescended to fall wounded to the ground but rose again, like Antaeus, and cleared all before me. I borrowed from George Rodgers, who was a few years older than me, his Sheriff Repeating Pistol. It shone like silver and was made out of the fragile pot-metal that went into children's toys of that sort. And one fearful day, when I fell wounded on a concrete path, the pistol fell out of my hand and was shattered into pieces. Reality in all its horror descended on me. In tears I went to the kindly lady, the mother of the man who owned the pistol, to plead my case for me. And she forgave me, and so did George, a most magnanimous man.

But a dream had been shattered with the pistol. I knew then that I was not Harry Carey, that I had never shot a single robber, that – God help us all – perhaps Harry Carey had never existed. And that even if he had, he had never made that hero's leap through the roof of the bank.

Years later I saw that he was still alive and playing in some Western movie. And feeling something of what I had felt when I went with Annie and my sister Kathleen to see *Soft Shoes*, I went to see him again. He was in a very minor role. He was a stiff old man.

And there went another dream.

Brenda Gannon

On a visit to Dingle in 1984 I went to the local cinema to see Al Pacino in *Scarface*. As the cinema filled up around me and the trailers were screened, one of the town 'characters' stood up abruptly and walked out. A few minutes later he returned carrying a violin case. Because this was a gangster film, the audience was curious as to what the case contained. About five or ten minutes into the film, as the tension on screen was mounting, the guy jumped up from his seat. Everyone turned to see what was happening just as he threw the case open and started throwing sweets around the audience.

Sam McAughtry

I am old enough to have gone to the pictures when they were silent. I remember seeing *The Jazz Singer* in the Duncairn Cinema in Belfast, and hearing Al Jolson speak the famous words.

I can remember being frightened by a 'haunted house' film – a comedy in which, I think, Chester Conklin's white coat got caught on a coat rack, and he dragged it behind him and thought it was following him. I was terrified. I suppose I would have been about five.

We had several picture houses in North Belfast that catered for the bottom layer of society – wooden forms, a heavy application of disinfectant to overcome the effect of hundreds of little boys peeing on the floor, attendants who handed out thick ears, and certain boys barred from entering because of past misdeeds. The nearest one to us was the Midland, named after the nearby Midland railway station. We called it 'Joe's' because it was owed by a Mr Joe McKibben.

We had variety stage acts as well as the films. The numbered tickets were held on to, because a prize draw for one shilling was made. My most vivid memory is of winning the shilling, going on stage to collect it, then having to fight off a dozen individual hold-up men as I made my way out of Joe's with the cash – forget about the picture! Another recollection is of the serious number of injuries – falling from trees in the park and banisters at home – that followed the first Johnny Weissmuller/Maureen O'Sullivan version of *Tarzan of the Apes*.

Mary O'Rourke, TD
Cinema and the Power of the Younger Sibling

I can vividly recall the Aladdin's Cave that was the glittery glory of the Ritz cinema in Athlone.

My sister Ann and my brother Paddy used to make arrangements to meet their respective boyfriend and girlfriend at the cinema for the Saturday afternoon matinée, on the condition (laid down by my mother) that they would have to bring me along to keep me occupied. Neither needed me tagging along keeping an eye on them while they met their respective partners – a fact I was clever enough to appreciate! I brazenly asked both how much it was worth to them to keep my mouth shut. Ann used to get particularly annoyed: she was the sophisticate, thrilled to be brought to the pictures by the boyfriend, whilst Paddy, much more laid-back about the situation, knew he was being got at by his seven-year-old sister and gave me a couple of pence to keep my mouth shut.

I particularly remember going to see *Tarzan*: collecting my usual hush-money before entering the local cinema, I packed up on goodies for the film and sat near the front while Paddy, Ann and their opposite numbers got as close to the back rows of the cinema as possible. On the way home that evening, however, I threatened Ann that I was going to tell our mother that she had been at the cinema with her boyfriend. Ann first promised all types of retribution, but when that failed to have the desired effect, she switched to pleading with me to keep quiet:

She: 'You can do anything to me.'

Me: 'I want to kick you.'

She agreed that I could, and there and then I did.

Thereafter, many times at home on these Saturday evenings, I'd stand behind my mother, looking over her head at Ann and Paddy, miming telling about their liaisons in the cinema. Although I never did, I had a terrible power over them for those few years. They paid in full for their innocent pleasures.

John Quinn
For One Night Only

Sikey Dunne set up a picture-show each Sunday night
In Sherrock's garage.
'Next attraction – James Cagney in WHITE HEAT –
For one night only – full supporting programme –
Eight-thirty pm SHARP!'
(In other words, no dawdling after devotions, folks)
Dawdle?
We shed our surplices and candle-greased soutanes
With unholy zest
And scuttled down the street
Lured by the siren strains of Rosie Clooney's
'Comeonamyhouseamyhouse'
Deserting God for a shilling dose of Mammon,
And there, careless of grease-pocked wooden seats
Oil-soaked sawdust and icy draughts
We surrendered to the celluloid world
And warmed in the glow of Cagney's *White Heat*.

Later we fought a famous gunbattle in the shadowy street
Dropped into 'Sam's' for bourbon with ice
Slapped Mickey Fagan behind bars
And raced off home as he whined
'You guys can't pin this rap on ME!'

Next morning in the frosty light
There was no Plaza or Savoy, but Sherrock's Garage
And Manhattan Sam stood stiffly with his regulation
County Council coat of straw.
Someone had sprung Mickey Fagan too –
The heavy church gates lay open
As we trooped back to serve our other Master.
(Mass begins at 7:30 am SHARP, said Father Farrell)
But Jimmy Cagney had blazed into our lives
For one night only.

CINEMA PARADISO

Lelia Doolan
Nights at the Opera; or, I Fell into the Butter

My two older brothers, Jim and Paddy, started me off. Up onto the bar of Jim's bike and off down to St Mary's College, Rathmines, on a Sunday afternoon. A huge noisy hall, hundreds of small legs and arms waving, barely perched on schoolroom chairs; chinks of light high up under the almost-fitting blinds and men in long black frocks who were called Sir or Father, fixing a funny-looking machine.

And then blackness and whirring and a hush among the babblers, and a blur up high on the big white sheet and, suddenly, music and faces and real people moving around on the sheet. Mystery, fascination, tremendous absorption. And hilarity. *A Night at the Opera* was the film, the first voyage into other worlds.

We went home and told our parents the whole story, with actions, at the tea-table in the kitchen. I'm sure they couldn't make head or tail of it, but we laughed so much we fell into the butter.

Since then, the years of addiction have had their moments and places – the Stella in Rathmines, the Classic in Terenure, terror in the Metropole at the graveyard scene in *Great Expectations*; serious aversion to *Bambi* (was it at the Astor?); as a student, scraping the money together, parking the bike in O'Connell Street, green raffle ticket in the handlebars, lies to the mother about working in the library, and bingeing on a Friday diet of four films one after another. The Adelphi at 2:05; the Capitol at 4:20 (including floor show); 6:30 at the Regal Rooms; Tommy Dando and the big picture at the Savoy at 8:20. Elevenpence a ticket.

Memories of my brother Matt racily narrating film stories to relieve the strains of haymaking in Co. Clare; memories of the companionable dark at Queen's Theatre in Belfast, in now-defunct cinemas in Westport, Belmullet, Ennis – and in the palace of dreams: the Claddagh in Galway. All the emotions arise, loosening mind and limbs – tension and fear and pity, and laughter falling into the butter.

Mary Harney

I didn't often go to the cinema as a child. It was a very rare experience and perhaps its very rarity made it all the more memorable.

My earliest recollection of going to the pictures is of a family Christmas treat when my parents took myself and my brothers to see *Robin Hood and his Merry Men*. I was about nine years old at the time and I remember the experience with a lot of pleasure – the journey into town (the film was showing in the old Ambassador cinema at the top of O'Connell Street); queuing to purchase the tickets (we didn't even feel the cold); my first taste of an Orange Maid, that extra large and rather expensive orange ice-pop that one could only purchase in the cinema. And the film itself was everything a child could wish to see. Of course compared to productions of the same film in the 90s I realise now that Friar Tuck, Little John and company were extraordinarily clean for outlaws living in Sherwood Forest in the Middle Ages; but Robin Hood stole from the rich to give to the poor, the Sheriff of Nottingham was suitably evil and Maid Marian provided the 'romantic' interest. I still think this film was better entertainment than Kevin Costner's much later offering.

There were of course a number of trips to the cinema during my schooldays, to see biblical epics such as *Ben Hur* and *King of Kings* and a film much favoured by the nuns who taught us – *The Song of Bernadette*. These were also magical occasions; even having to wear a school uniform didn't detract from them. Performing chores at home to gain some extra spending money for these outings is also a big part of my childhood memories. I can still remember the joy of being able to afford those lovely big bags of popcorn.

As a young adult my trips to the cinema became more frequent, and musicals such as *April Love*, *Oklahoma* and *Seven Brides for Seven Brothers* were firm favourites. The film I enjoyed most during my adolescence was *The King and I* – in fact I am sure I saw it no less than four times.

In later years, as my political career took off and Dáil and constituency commitments intensified, my trips to the cinema became even rarer than they were in childhood. The advent of video recorders has made me lazy about organising film outings. One of my more recent trips to the cinema was a couple of years ago to see Jodie Foster's very fine film *The Accused*.

I think that one of the things that made the cinema special in my childhood was the sheer magic and mystery of it all. Like all children then, I had absolutely no idea how films were made, nor was I in any way curious about the technical details; it was more than enough to just watch a film. I well remember that I was always impatient for the film to end just so that I would know the full story – was the ending sad, happy or inconclusive? Perhaps the relative lack of pre-release hype such as that associated with *Jurassic Park* or this summer's *The Hunchback of Notre Dame* made those trips to the cinema so memorable. There were no great expectations beforehand, and therefore no sense of disappointment afterwards – except that I was always depressed if the film ended sadly and wondered for weeks what happened if it was inconclusive.

Louis Marcus

When I was a boy in Cork, I went every afternoon to what were known as 'the pitchers'. The city was full of cinemas then.

The Savoy was huge, opulently decorated in Venetian style. The Palace retained the gilt proscenium and curved red-velvet boxes of a Victorian music-hall. The Pavilion had a cream marble frontage; there was something Moorish about the Lee and sparely modern about the Ritz. I was once in the Assembly Rooms, where you sat on hard benches. But nice boys like me didn't go to the Coliseum, the Imperial or the Lido, which reputedly accepted jam-jars for admission. Some of these houses suffered, or perhaps enjoyed, the effects of Corkonian abbreviation – the Pav, the Col and the Assems.

The Capitol, now the only commercial cinema in Cork, was a late arrival. It boasted a restaurant; but so did the Pavilion and the Savoy. The latter, indeed, was a favourite place for meetings of all sorts over coffee. It was there I played chess in the Bellevue Club, attended my first meetings of the Cork Branch of the Irish Film Society, and experienced, as a guest, a grotesque meeting of the Cork Communist Party.

There was rigorous censorship of films but no age certificates. So while adults could not see anything with a hint of adultery, young boys like myself could watch thrillers of unspeakable horror. I still shudder at *The Upturned Glass*, with James Mason and his one-time wife, Pamela Kellino; and *Green for Danger*, with its hospital serial killer masked like a surgeon, has left me with a lifelong antipathy to operating theatres.

When I was old enough to go to the pictures at night, I learned the tricks of the 'continuous performance'. There were no breaks between shows and people took their seats whenever they arrived. So by the last performance, when you were likely to have a girl with you, you stood against the side wall waiting for some seated patrons to experience *déjà vu*, mutter 'this is where we came in' and vacate the premises.

Another side effect of the continuous performance was that people would arrange to meet inside rather than outside the cinema. That way, the earlycomer could be enjoying the show and the latecomer, on entering, would cry out the name of the friend to discover his location. I remember a science-fiction horror film where two policemen are nervously searching some darkened tunnels for a sinister alien creature. Suddenly, one of them realises he is alone. He begins to cry out for his companion, more and more anxiously – 'Where are you? Where are you?'

From the gods of the Savoy came the answering call: 'I'm up here in de wan-an-nines!'

David Norris
Magic

For a race of dreamers like the Irish, the cinema has always had a strong fascination. Even in the 60s and 70s, when everyone said the cinema was finished or would shortly be finished by the rival entertainments of television, the Irish public remained faithful to the celluloid dream, the week-ends in Dublin still saw cinema queues entertained by buskers.

Of course, when I was young it seemed to me that there were many more cinemas – cinemas of the old type, divided into a kind of social hierarchy. There were good strongly middle-class city-centre cinemas, like the Metropole, the Savoy, and the Regal Rooms, which showed serious films, family films, Shakespearean drama. Slightly lower down were the Carlton and the Adelphi. The Carlton specialised in blood-dripping horror, *Dracula* and *The Curse of the Mummy's Tomb*, and gangster stories like *The Rise and Fall of Legs Diamond*, in which mobsters careered around the streets of Chicago and New York in wonderfully old-fashioned cars, peppering restaurants with machine-gun bullets and managing to look dashing all the time as their black-and-white images flickered across the screen.

In a class of its own was the Royal, the largest cinema theatre in Dublin, which I only occasionally visited but of which I have fond memories. Entertainment there was a real bargain. You got not just a full cinema programme, but also a stage show, which usually included Tommy Dando, hoisted electrically into view, sitting astride an enormous Wurlitzer organ as he played his signature tune, 'Keep Your Sunny Side Up'. Then would follow community singing with a vast auditorium swaying and rocking, everyone joining in good-humouredly; those of us who couldn't quite recall the words of the popular songs (which were even then out of date, like 'Daisy, Daisy... on a Bicycle Made for Two') had the assistance of the words projected onto a screen, with a little pinpoint of light bouncing across the words to indicate exactly where we were in the song.

The stage show featured the Royalettes, a group of high-kicking formation dancers who seemed to us ineffably glamorous, echoes of New York and Paris and London, the Radio City Music Hall, the Bluebell Girls and the Folies Bergères. In addition to romance, our appetite for comedy was satisfied by routines provided by Jimmy O'Dea, Maureen Potter, Danny Cummins, Cecil Sheridan and the rest. I don't think we realised what good value this was for about half a crown – half a dollar, two and a kick, as we used to call those now-vanished coins; less than fifteen pence in the new money. Some of the cinemas also had restaurants – like the Metropole, which was a huge complex, including a enormous bar and a ballroom as well as a restaurant upstairs, where, if you were really lucky on birthdays, you were treated to a meal which somehow always included chips and ice cream.

Going to the cinema in those days was a full-blown experience. There were no economy measures, no squalid little boxes created out of the ruins of a larger cinema from which five or six antiseptically-numbered viewing chambers have been created. These were cinema palaces decorated in styles that echoed the Moorish and Egyptian fantasies of Hollywood. When the show started house lights dimmed, spotlights shone for a moment on the effect of minarets and casemented windows, and then those wonderfully diaphanous silken curtains changed like the aurora borealis under the projection lights from pink to green as they parted to show what looked like a cockleshell opening to reveal a shamrock displaying a logo for Cinema and General Publicity, which meant we were in for all the beloved and ridiculed ads such as that in which a pair of women's elegant legs emerged in high heels from a mirror while a breathy voiceover uttered the slogan 'Legs look lovelier in Bradmola'.

When the advertisements were over, the crowing of a black and white cock on the screen announced the 'Pathe News'. In those days the clipped British tone of the newsreader still spoke of the Empire and its far-flung outposts and often carried news of the young Queen, who was ushering in a new Elizabethan Age across the water. But there were also items of more interest to the Irish public – the Pope carried in procession across St Peter's Square on a throne with great peacock fans like some pagan god, or the GAA All-Ireland final in Croke Park, with a commentary by one of the unforgettable voices of Ireland, Mícheál Ó hEithir. Then the curtains closed again, the house lights went up and at each side of the screen spotlights came on, focusing on a pair of young women with wooden trays strapped over their shoulders, looking like escapees from a British holiday camp with their cocky little hats and uniforms. These were the Orange Maid girls and they sold ice cream in tubs with little wooden spoons, bags of popcorn, bars of chocolate and boxes of smarties and fruit gums. Their duty done, they retired. The cinema went dark again and the curtains were parting once more, this time for the main feature.

Frequently this was a product of the J. Arthur Rank Studios, and so, after the initial frames showing the censor's certificate in Irish, the next image was the sweaty torso of a muscle-man as he flexed backwards, a giant drumstick in his hand, to strike the enormous gong. *The Titfield Thunderbolt* or one of the great classics of the British cinema was sometimes followed, if we were lucky, by a second feature, a crime story. *Fabian of the Yard* was introduced, if my memory serves me right, by the sepulchral tones of Edger Lustgarten, who dissected the crime and demonstrated that in the long run this profession rarely paid. The cinema was very moral in those days, at least in Ireland.

The cinema was often a Saturday afternoon treat in the Dublin of my childhood, and I remember well how we were so imaginatively and emotionally engaged with the doings on the screen that when we staggered out into the new sunlight of O'Connell Street from the womb of the cinema it was Dublin's reality that seemed the illusion and not the still warm world of fantasy that we left behind. There was music too in those days. Not the quadraphonic sound, explosions, wallops and crumps to which we are now treated. This was the age of Mantovani, 'The Lonely Ballerina', Manuel and his 'Music of the Mountain'. The bigger cinemas had impressive ticket kiosks where, when you proffered your money, the tickets came up through a little metallic grill by magic. There were usherettes with torches, doormen and commissionaires in gorgeous braided uniforms and hats like officers from some Ruritanian army.

There were some older-style cinemas too – the Grafton, in Grafton Street, had been one of the early cinemas in which the silent films had been shown to the accompaniment of tinkling piano music. Indeed, across the street in Cavendish's furniture shop the late Peggy Dell still valiantly tickled the ivories, a cigarette dangling from her lips as she played ragtime and swing. In the 60s the Grafton cinema became for a time a news and cartoon cinema, and it too had a small restaurant upstairs where poetic types gathered to discuss the state of their souls. The suburbs had their cinemas too. Rathmines had the ancient Princess Cinema, a survivor from the 20s, and the Stella, where schoolboys often took their first dates. At the lower end of the scale there were cinemas like the Regal, Ringsend, to which admission was reputed to be sixpence and a jam jar, and where legend had it that if you were not careful you would get fleas – just as it was commonly supposed that you could get VD from a lavatory seat, although I never came across casualties in either circumstance. The only thing I remember from my one visit to the Regal to see a cowboy film was the enthusiastic way in which the largely juvenile audience interacted with the performance on screen and, when they were bored, played tip and tag among the seats to the distress of the elderly commissionaire and usherette.

I have affectionate memories of my own local cinema, the Ritz in Serpentine Avenue, Ballsbridge, to which we used to trudge, along a little path (now closed) beside the railway line, nursing our sunburn on summer evenings to see Ealing comedies like *The Lady Killers*, or *The Lavender Hill Mob* with Alec Guinness (before he was knighted) and Bernard Cribbens, or the early Carry On films. There was an innocent charm about those days and that real, if almost totally sexless, comedy.

Being a good little Church of Ireland boy, I did not normally attend the cinema on Sunday. One memorable Sunday I escaped with some Roman Catholic friends and went to the Regent cinema in Blackrock. I had my reward. The programme for that day consisted of a melodrama about a mad Nazi scientist who had escaped after the war and was conducting a series of underground experiments of a biological nature, related somehow to German warfare, on a set of innocent victims. My horror of injections and all kind of medical procedures made me squirm in misery rather than pleasure as the lurid story unfolded. I had told my mother that I was going for an improving walk. She found it difficult to understand my nightmares, as for the next week I nightly regurgitated the horrors of the screen.

Perhaps it is middle age setting in, but cinema doesn't seem to me to have the automatic sense of adventure and glamour that it did when I was young. One can sometimes recapture this feeling – as I did quite recently on my first visit to the Irish Film Centre in Temple Bar. Here again was the atmosphere I enjoyed as a child, the sense of adventure, the treat – although instead of plush button banquette and a restaurant with heavy cutlery and heavier china, there was a snack bar and a soda fountain. There was still, in that glorious environment, real cinema. And so I hope that the young people of this generation will experience in their own way the magic of the cinema as it was made available to me in Dublin twenty, thirty, even forty golden years ago, when the Metropole, the Regal Rooms and the Capital reigned supreme in Dublin.

Jimmy Lacey

Cinema:
'Truth 24 times a second.' – Jean-Luc Godard
'A ribbon of dreams.' – Orson Welles
'A waste of good drinking time.' – my Uncle Joe

Ah! the pictures! All things to all men. To me it was everything. Yes, now it can be told, the naked truth... nailed to the page! I was a ten-pictures-a-week man. But I could handle it. My appetite for all things Hollywood was insatiable. Coonskin-capped and whistling 'Colonel Bogey's March', I would swap chewing-gum film-star cards while queuing outside Wexford's Capitol cinema for my afternoon fix. This was topped by a nightly double shot of Randolph Scott and 'The Dook' (John Wayne) – followed by an under-the-sheets *Picture Show Annual* by flashlight until the sandman came.

But in the Wexford of the 50s and 60s, a pictures-mad town, my beautiful addiction went virtually unnoticed. I was surrounded by fellow victims: the butcher, the baker, the wealthy bookmaker, all hopelessly hooked. Even our postman would always ring twice. Wexford, the magical kingdom by the sea, boasted three cinemas with double bills which changed four times a week. So in any given seven days it was possible to take in a staggering fifteen to twenty films. The demand for nightly escape was so great that a backlog of revivals was shown to satisfy the cravings of the cinematically-damned. As late as the mid-60s you could still catch old Warner Bros. Bogart pictures at the Abbey, the Capitol or the Cinema Palace. In fact, on the night of November 23rd 1963, ashen-faced creatures emerged from a showing of *White Heat*, shell-shocked at the news of the cutting down of our very own boy-saint American president.

At the time there seemed to be a cinematic evocation to suit every occasion. Teachers warned us of ending up 'like killer Dino'. A hard chaw was referred to as 'The King of the Khyber Rifles going around'. Less than truthful children were promised Pinocchio's nose. One dreary CBS day while lost in an under-the-desk 'Photoplay', I was nabbed red-handed by Brother 'Bulldog' Malone. Waving his one snot-free sleeve in my direction, he delivered unto me the following chilly forecast: 'Lacey, with yer Tony Curtis pants and the butt hanging out of yer lip, you're bound for Anne Street corner' (the location of the local dole office).

People were re-christened after the stars. The projectionist in the Cinema Palace so loved the various wide-screen processes that he came to be known as Vista – or, on formal occasions, Mister Vision. One poor deluded creature was so taken with the now-forgotten Rory Calhoun Z-grade quickie, *The Saga of Hemp Brown*, that he adopted the title and would answer to no other. He would greet us with the immortal catch-phrase 'Hemp Brown is in town'. A local priest called Father Jordan was named Flash (though not to his face). A hermit type who seldom ventured out into the world became Boo Radley. And in the age of the spaghetti Western, two members of an accident-prone family received the ultimate accolade. The younger brother took a tumble from the gasworks wall, recovering to obtain a rather handsome financial compensation. Shortly thereafter Brother No. 2, while erecting a rooftop aerial, also fell to earth. Surviving smashed limbs, he nabbed a larger settlement on the big compo. They passed into Wexford lore as, respectively, A Fistful of Dollars and For A Few Dollars More. And to this day there's a DUKE Connors, a BORIS Carrol, a CROCKETT Clancy, a MUGS Cleere and a SACH O'Connor (the Bowery Boys were big in Wexford).

And it always stunned me how cine-literate your average John Doe could be. The Tony-Curtis-trousered Anne-Streeter could, at the drop of a sombrero, reel off the collected works of Dan Duryea, between drags on his Craven A. Heathens who were stumped by the seven deadly sins, the Ten Commandments or the three mysteries of Fatima could effortlessly rattle off the names of all the Dead End Kids, the Twelve Angry Men and the Magnificent Seven (the trick is to think of Brad Dexter first). And many's the large bottle that was won in wagers by recalling Al Mancini as the forgotten one of the Dirty Dozen.

And always the song. For days after *Calamity Jane* played the Abbey, the whole town whistled 'The Deadwood Stage' ('Whipcrack away, whipcrack away, whipcrack awaaaaayyy'). And we all knew, courtesy of Jimmy Young, that 'No oul hoot/could ever outshoot/the Man from Laram-eeeeee!' Undisputed musical hero of the day was Frankie Laine. Frankie was involved in *The Gunfight At the OK Corral*, took *The 3:10 To Yuma* and begged his darlin' not to forsake him at *High Noon*. The theme song to *Davy Crockett, King of the Wild Frontier* was quickly hijacked by fans of Wexford's legendary hurlers to become 'Nicky Rackard, King of the Close-In Free' (and can still be heard ringing from Wexford alehouses on special occasions). And in the chicken-and-egg scenario of *The Legend of Tom Dooley*, the song begat the film. The ad in the *Wexford Free Press* ran: 'Out of THAT song, a fury of a movie...hear the Kingston Trio sing.' We did.

I was always a sucker for the corny selling line in the local paper and can still recall the weekly hyperbole. 'These are the young and the damned who grow in the cracks of the concrete jungle' screamed the tag line for *The Young Savages*. Obviously aware of Joe Punter's aversion to films 'with writing on the bottom', the publicity for *Bernadette of Lourdes* reassuringly stated 'Filmed entirely at Lourdes with the blessing of Pope John XXIII. This film is NOT subtitled.' I'll never forget the threat that accompanied the arrival of *Ben Hur*: 'Latecomers not admitted until completion of beautiful nativity prologue.' But I (in hindsight) suspect the hand of Hitchcock rather than the local manager in *Psycho*'s 'Please don't give away the ending, it's the only one we've got.'

I always felt gypped by the contradiction-in-terms promise of 'a Scotland Yard thriller'. English films were not popular. One glance at the muscular chap banging the gong elicited the collective groan of 'Oh no! An English picture.' However, we would endure the dull stiffness of a British Lion film to catch a glimpse of our own John Welsh. Oh yes, in Wexford we had our very own movie stars, and many's the grey after-noon we queued to see John 'Sandy' Welsh in such classics as *The Clue of the Missing Ape*, *Man in the Shadow* or *The Case of Soho Red*. And what of the mighty Dan O'Herlihy? Sure wasn't he from Hill Street? And wasn't he up for the Oscar for *The Adventures of Robinson Crusoe*? I could never figure out how, in Wexford, everybody's Da went to school with Danny Boy. Even my own family got in on the act, with dear papa working as an extra on *Moby Dick* and *Shake Hands with the Devil*.

The passage of time could be gauged by the topicality of the films on show. *Rock Around the Clock* became *Twist Around the Clock*. The Tony Curtis pants gave way to red-tab Levis in the age of Bond and the Beatles. Brando and Marilyn were supplanted by Clint and La Cardinale. And in THAT summer, I saw no contradiction in sporting an explosion-in-a-paint-factory kaftan while cheering on the beautiful Dunaway and Beatty's killing spree in *Bonnie and Clyde*. My own double-barrelled state of mind was echoed in that film's tag-line – 'They're young, they're in love and they kill people.'

One sad day in the early 70s, Vista the projectionist crashed his Honda 50 and the Cinema Palace closed its doors forever. It was that simple. Eat your heart out Larry McMurty. In the dying days of the Capitol we were treated to the delightfully surreal Michelangelo Antonioni/Joe Lynch double-bill of *The Passenger* and *Never Mind the Quality, Feel the Width*. The writing was surely on the wall now. By the time the Abbey bit the dust, to be replaced by our bright shiny new cineplex, the golden age of picture-going in Wexford had long since passed.

A hundred years of cinema? During my youth, I lived a hundred years a night in the picture palaces of Wexford.

Ray Bates

My memories of early cinema-going in Dublin date from just after the time when an admission fee of six jam-jars was not as unusual as it might sound today. But I do remember in the early 50s paying 3d (or 1p now) every Sunday to sit in the 'woodeners' at the front of the Broadway Cinema in Manor Street, while the more affluent patrons sat in the 'cushioners' behind us. The programmes were classic fare for the time: trailer; short; 'follower-upper'; and the 'big picture'. I freely admit to adding to the noisy impatience during the 'talky bits' and the 'love bits' that dragged on between the 'action bits' when we cheered the 'chap' and booed the 'baddy'. And yes, I remember re-enacting the more dramatic moments as a gang of us returned home at six o'clock, when parked cars became encircled covered wagons and startled passers-by became renegade Indians.

'Permanent seats' seem to have disappeared from the scene sometime in the 60s, but forty years ago, I had an Aunt Sadie who was the proud possessor of two such seats in the Savoy – when it was all one monolithic cinema capable of holding thousands of people. They weren't actually permanent – you paid in advance for a year, and two specific seats became 'yours' for that duration. I don't remember thinking that the fact my aunt had these seats was in any way extraordinary. She was no dowager; she simply led an ordered life, loved the cinema and went to it every week. This was at a time when it was unusual for cinemas to show the same film for more than a week. When these status symbols couldn't be used by my aunt for whatever reason (usually the fact that a film she'd already seen had been held over for a second week), my mother would automatically inherit the seats and I would be brought down-town as a special treat.

The Savoy was also the venue I chose for my Confirmation Day outing in 1959. Elvis Presley was starring in *Jailhouse Rock* and nothing less than a visit would satisfy me for my big day. This outing must have sounded a little incongruous, in comparison to my schoolmates' activities, when our teacher asked each of us to describe how we had spent our Confirmation Day.

My abiding memory of walking out of the Savoy, especially when it was a non-stop show (that is, one went in in the middle of the picture, and left when that bit came around again), is of the incredible clouds of smoke caught in the projector beams – everybody smoked in those days.

As we grew older we were allowed to venture further afield on our own – to the Bohemian Cinema in Phibsboro and later to the State Cinema, when it opened. I remember going to the first film shown in the State – *Twenty Thousand Leagues Under the Sea* – all about divers, sponges and octopuses.

I have always been completely impervious to horror movies, but when I was about six I remember crying with terror at – of all films – *Pinocchio*. When the nasty fox fed them the drink that turned them into donkeys while they were playing snooker, I was inconsolable. Even to this day, when I see a rerun of the film I get a flashback to my six-year-old experience.

I remember being at the 'old' Royal in the 50s, where we used to sit through the film, followed by a live variety show, followed by the film again. It involved a full day out, with a 'picnic' of bananas and chocolates consumed between the stage show and the film. Nowadays, I often bemoan the passing of the non-stop performance. With no clear-out of patrons between shows you were able to see the bit you missed and even stay on for a second viewing.

When I was about ten, I remember going to the 'old' Regal where I saw *The Blue Angel*. I was obviously too young to appreciate what was going on, but nonetheless I knew that simply being there was indulging in some kind of forbidden fruit. There followed a period in my teens where the opposite sex entered the frame and the celluloid on the silver screen paled into insignificance when compared with the real activities in the stalls. And, on the way home, the retelling – if not re-enactment – of real and sometimes exaggerated happenings in the cinema echoed, in retrospect, the return journey of our gang from the Broadway cimema in the 50s.

Gerry Stembridge
in conversation

I do have a particular memory of the first time I went to the pictures and the story that surrounds it. I must only have been six or seven. I pestered my mother to let me go and see *Darby O'Gill and the Little People*: it was the kind of film everybody would have been talking about at the time. That was fine, so my older brother,who was about eleven years old (he was 'a big boy'), was assigned to bring me. He and I met up with friends of his to go to the pictures. It transpired, however, that he and his friends didn't want to see *Darby O'Gill and the Little People*. They wanted to go see the Christopher Lee *Dracula*. I was left out of the equation. Obviously I was very disappointed, but there was a little frisson about the idea of going to see *Dracula* as well. When I think about it – they let a seven-year-old in to see *Dracula*. Down the country in those days, the ratings didn't matter a huge amount. If you were anywhere within the region of the age there was no problem.

So *Dracula* was the first film I saw. The best thing about it was that my brother was worried about me letting the cat out of the bag to my mother. So on the way home, as well as warning me not to tell her, he brought me round to the cinema where *Darby O'Gill and the Little People* was playing and showed me stills from the film, so I would have something to latch onto if my mother questioned me. And I lied to my mother. 'What was it like, what was it about?' and I conjured up whatever images had been shown in the stills. Mind you, it did mean that I didn't get to see *Darby O'Gill and the Little People* for years after that: because I'd supposedly just seen it, I could hardly ask to see it again. On the other hand, I've always had an affection for that version of *Dracula*.

When I started going to the pictures, there were six cinemas in Limerick, all with distinguishing features. There was the Lyric; even as a kid, you knew the Lyric was a low-rent cinema, because it had wooden benches in the front half and it cost 3d for the matinée. *Hercules* films and stuff starring Steve Reeves seemed to be the mainstay of the Lyric. When I think about it, the first part of my film-going, the late 60s, was a really crap time for films. What's more, it used to take a very long time for any kind of picture to get to Limerick (except to the Savoy), so even that crap tended to be four or five years out of date. Anyway, then there was the Royal, which is still there as some kind of concert venue. The distinguishing feature of the Royal was that you entered behind the screen. There was always something weird about it, because if you arrived late you were very aware that you were on view. The last of the cheap cinemas was the City Theatre, which you can't really count because it was only a part-time cinema, doing Saturday matinées. They did have a fad for giving away sweets with the cinema tickets (I specifically remember getting a packet of fruit pastilles) to bring kids in. It didn't especially work.

Then there were the three classier cinemas. In grade two were the Carlton and the Grand Central. (We obviously stole the cinema names from Dublin.) They were decent enough cinemas and would always get first-run films. They're both gone now. The Carlton was hanging in there until very recently, when the Savoy turned itself into a six-screen multiplex. My godfather uncle was a projectionist in the Grand Central and I occasionally got to go into the projection room, so I have some claims to a *Cinema Paradiso* background. I remember thinking that it was brilliant and that my godfather had a really important job, that he was at the centre of the movie industry. He loved it. He died just a few years ago – pretty much around the time they were knocking down the old Savoy. The Savoy was the final one. It got all the prime films. It was a beautifully ornate 1930s picture palace, with the odd feature that the stalls only went as far back as where the balcony started; then there was this kind of riser and the balcony started separately – so everybody in the stalls could turn around and look at the rich people in the balcony who had paid extra.

What I wonder today is how going to the pictures might have influenced my writing. I'm not sure how serious I am about this, but when I was thirteen or fourteen, I'd frequently go to the pictures when I got out of school at four o'clock. I always loved going on my own more than going with a bunch of friends; I just loved sitting there in the dark. But I wouldn't hang around town waiting for the next performance to start – I just paid my money and went in. So I've a lot of memories of going into films which were already well under way. 'We must see it from the beginning' wasn't a feature of my childhood. People at the box office might mention it, but it was no big deal. Going to the pictures was in no way an artistic or intellectual enterprise. So I'd quite happily watch the second half of a film, then stay and watch the first half (and sometimes the whole film again if I liked it enough).

I wonder how that affected my way of thinking about the way things are structured? In my own writing, both in theatre and in film, structure is very important to me and I do quite an amount of playing with time. Having got used to watching a story conclude and then going back and saying 'Ah, that's what was going on when they were doing that', I wonder – will I ever be able to write a linear story?

Harvey O'Brien
Opening Night

On Saturday 16 December 1950, an advertisement appeared in the *Clare Champion* declaring the grand opening of the Mars Cinema in Kilrush at 8:30 pm the following evening. On Sunday morning the seating had not yet been installed, and at 10 am a group of local volunteers – including Charles Glynn, Bryan O'Doherty, James McGuane, local tradesmen Jack Keller (who also erected the screen) and Colman – began screwdriving them in. The last balcony seat was fastened at 8 pm and the show went ahead as scheduled. For their efforts, the volunteers were rewarded with a barrel of porter.

The opening was attended by a capacity crowd, and blessed by the local parish priest, the Very Rev. Canon Meade. The film was *Mr Belvedere Goes to College* (1949) with Clifton Webb and Shirley Temple, and admissions were 1/8d, 1/3d and 8d.

The *Clare Champion* of 23 December 1950 reported:

'There was an exceptionally large number of people at the opening of the new Mars Cinema at Frances St. on Sunday night, and everyone was thoroughly satisfied with the programme and also with the arrangements made for the comfort of patrons. The new cinema is situated in the principal street of Kilrush and is capable of accommodating 850 persons. It is well lighted with comfortable seating accommodation, and reckoned by experts to rank among the finest cinemas in Munster.'

Bill Hughes

Bette Davis turned around slowly from the drinks cabinet and her lover's head came tumbling down the stairs. The camera crash-zoomed to her distorted mouth as she screamed in terror.

I went into shock and wet my pants.

I was twelve and the film, *Hush Hush Sweet Charlotte*, was definitely of the over-18s variety.

I grew up in Athy, County Kildare, where the Grove cinema nestles against the railway bridge just across the tracks from the town's old graveyard. The family drapery shop on Leinster Street had a glass door, the perfect poster site for the cinema to advertise the next week's attractions, and giving us a free pass guaranteed them this prime spot. In hindsight I suppose it was just luck that I got the pass nine times out of ten, since my seven brothers and five sisters didn't share my addiction to sitting in the dark watching the big screen.

The poster always arrived on Friday afternoons, so my first stop when I got home from school was to press the 'cash-total' button on the till and rummage under the pound notes to see where my mother had hidden the little white cardboard slip with the date on it. *Dracula*, *Frankenstein* and Noel Purcell were instant turnoffs so the pass would go back in the till. Any thriller, Western or war film, however, meant a fight with my older brother – which I happily lost, since he had hurling and football practice four nights a week which usually meant he couldn't use the pass anyway. Those weeks I got it by default. Musicals and foreign shit with subtitles were my undisputed domain.

I hated horror films but loved Bette Davis, and in those crucial years when the pass was my passport to heaven, she made some of the scariest horror films ever seen. Some were also amongst her campest work, but I was too young to appreciate it in those days. It was better to sit with my eyes shut tight, just listening to her voice crushing enemies and hoarsely mocking lovers.

One week the poster delivery boy left two passes stuck together, and the biggest decision was who was going to share my good fortune. As it happened, the passes were for Thursday night and I was to be senior altar boy at a Redemptorist Mission for the men of the parish. The priest seemed to go on forever and I resented every decade of the rosary, which he dragged out for full dramatic effect. One of my school friends was on bell duty, so I decided he should get the second ticket. He wasn't a regular picture-goer and it was a big deal.

Even though we raced off the altar ahead of the priest, we still missed the support feature, the newsreel and the ads and just barely made the trailer for James Bond in *Thunderball*. Neither of us knew anything about the film, *The Nightwalker*, except that it starred two of our favourites, Barbara Stanwyck and Robert Taylor, so it was bound to be brilliant. We couldn't have been more wrong.

God and the Redemptorist priest got their own back. In the first reel Barbara Stanwyck's husband, played by Robert Taylor, was killed in an explosion in their house, leaving her grief-stricken. When he started to appear in the middle of the night, beating a cane against her bedroom door with his eyes completely reversed and just the whites showing, my friend and I wished we hadn't come. As she got more terrified, he got more daring and broke into the bedroom and lifted her from the bed. My friend ended up sitting on my lap. We were screaming louder than

Barbara. It was an over-18s job again and we were both at the tender age of thirteen. After repeat pleas from the rest of the audience to shut up, we were eventually thrown out and told we were barred. I was crushed and blamed my friend for everything, but Jack, the cinema owner, lifted my barring order after a month.

The trouble with living in a small town, however, was that everybody knew everybody and the usherette was our housekeeper's best friend. My short-sighted defence in the wake of *The Nightwalker*, that they shouldn't have let me into an over-18s film in the first place, completely backfired two weeks later, when *Thunderball* finally came to town - with the dreaded 'adult' cert.

The Grove played a crucial role in the adolescence of the 60s genera-tion in Athy, supplying comfortable seats, low lighting and enough distraction on screen for no one to notice our arms slowly creeping around the girls next to us. Since everyone was doing it, however, it became a bit of a spectator sport and there were very few secrets that survived the searching eyes of the row behind. In Athy, all the great love stories started in the back row on Friday nights. Most relationships lasted the week, but some only lasted the length of the support feature. Fresh approaches were occasionally made in the queue for Taytos and ice pops, especially if the first date hadn't passed the snog test. Many times a girl's first sign of failure was when he came back from the shop with her sweets and took his jacket to move to another seat. In this small town that could only mean he was going to try another girl from her convent class or, worse still, a girl from the Tech. They were regarded as 'flyers'.

In those innocent times, it didn't take much to shock everybody. Snog-ging and groping were the limit of the Friday night romances, and so one piercing scream has become a legend in the town. As Max Von Sydow told Lazarus to come forth during the Easter holiday screening of The Greatest Story Ever Told, the cinema was rocked by a tearful plea in the dark: 'JESUS, CELINE, HE PUT HIS TONGUE IN MY MOUTH. AM I PREGNANT?'

Recently, the Grove re-opened as a multiscreen. I haven't been to see it yet. Part of me just wants to remember it as it used to be.

Kevin Rockett
A Bus Journey

At ten-to-two each Saturday the eagerly-awaited Kenneally's blue and white 'bone-shaker' double-decker bus arrived in the village of

Slieverue, three miles from Waterford on the New Ross road. The village combined Waterford Glass and Clover Meats worker-commuters with a rural backbone of small shopkeepers, publicans, farmers and agricultural workers. Despite its proximity to Waterford, the village was culturally set in Kilkenny, especially during the All-Ireland Hurling Championships. About this time, the sweetest of all victories, and for Slieverue the most wonderful of all celebrations, followed the 1957 final when three local players were members of Kilkenny's winning team.

The journey on Kenneally's bus to Waterford provided an unusual vista of the countryside for an eight-year-old. As it towered over the fields, it collected the regular groups of shoppers, children and teenagers, all released in their own way from supervised routines, which included clerical policing of selected screenings in the parochial hall, as they headed towards the freedom of the city.

On one such occasion when the bus stopped to pick up passengers in Ferrybank, socially and spiritually a suburb of Waterford despite being on the 'Kilkenny side' of the Suir, two young women continued with their conversation. 'So you're getting married next Saturday.'

'Yes.'

'Where did you meet him, then?'

An embarrassed silence.

'Well, at the fête in Mullinavat.'

Silence.

'What's he like?'

'Steady.'

If depression can visit an eight-year-old, then it descended on me at this moment. The short distance from Ferrybank to the Clock Tower had produced a vision of an adult world so constrained that the pleasure of a fête, of the marvellous, fabulous world of the village marquee, was reduced to 'steadiness' – a description that didn't sit easily with the appearance of the men seen in my family's pub at times of festivity and fêtes.

Alighting from the bus, the two women continued their intense discussion of trains, crinoline, and other materials that seemed more appropriate to the playground than the church, but which, apparently, were to be worn at the wedding. For my part, I dashed across the Quay to get away from such adult reality, and as always had enough time before the 'pictures' to explore the rich treasures of English comics in the newsagents and to feel the trivial trinkets in Woolworth's.

The children's community was re-formed at the cinema. There, children from the city and country bustled for the three o'clock show in an apparently democratic coming-together otherwise seen only in church or at a GAA match. As ever, though, there was a social hierarchy in the cinema, defined not just by front and back stalls, balcony and an area mysteriously called the 'parterre', but by the cinemas themselves. Between the 'fleapit' Coliseum at the end of the Quay and the Savoy and the Regina in the centre of the town was a social world, distinguished by the roughness of the former and the comfort of the latter. At the Regina and Savoy, the plush seats, carpeting, red velvet curtains, subdued lighting, and 'modern' music all contributed to an environment which felt sumptuous and sensuous when weighed against the standard lino and flagstones, naked lights or candles of most rural homes of the 1950s.

Eager anticipation gave way to awe when the enormous curtains were drawn, and the credit sequence was tolerated impatiently – an irony now much appreciated. Then in the darkness we were immersed in a world so different from our own, with sounds so rich, colours so vivid and varied and stories so extraordinary, that we experienced something that must have been what is now called 'magic realism'. John Wayne knocks down the door once more in a John Ford Western or in one of his Irish films, Davy Crockett explores the wild frontier, a nightclub owner or gangster is shot, we are frightened when the earth catches fire, a war plane comes directly at us from the screen... These were adventures unimaginable in the rote world of the classroom where tedium and lack of imagination dulled the senses.

We had no idea what film censorship was, unless we could relate the concept to denials of pleasure at home or in school. We didn't know then that almost all films assessed for release were cut or banned so that children of all ages could see them. This apparently generous policy by Ministers for Justice and Film Censors was, it seems, designed to maintain a child's view of the world into adulthood, but what it allowed children of the late 1950s and early 1960s was access to images unimaginable in the official culture.

After the emotionally-draining experience, we raced for the bus like members of the 7th Cavalry, as if trying to extend the cinema experience into the boring reality of the world. The bus journey home, a mere four hours after leaving the village, was more subdued as physical exhaustion took hold. The village itself was quiet by now, but the welcoming glow of home beckoned with a warmth richer than that of the cinema.

Sitting in the back seat of the Regina five years later, I discovered a different use for the cinema. Not, mind you, like at the Mullinavat fête – more like *To Have and Have Not* meets *In a Lonely Place*.

BRIEF ENCOUNTER

Evelyn Conlon
How about the truth?

It was January 10th, that I'm sure of, but I can't quite remember which year; early 60s, definitely. The town was Clones and the man was Michael. I wore a lime-green jersey wool pinafore made by my aunt, the V-neck hem a little puckered. The man was her brother-in-law and had asked her permission in an elegant Victorian manner. So here I was, sitting in the dark, the dark! I ask you, no one had told me. He put his arm around my shoulder and quite frankly I nearly passed out – at first I had thought that some weight had fallen on me from the ceiling, but because of the dark I couldn't see what it was. When the truth dawned on me I went rigid with fright. The poor fellow excused himself – probably thought this child was going to die on him – and when he came back he gave me a box of sweets. I couldn't touch even one of those Roses chocolates. We sat through the film, me terrified, him probably equally so, wondering what I would tell my aunt when I got back. He kept his arm to himself for the duration, I do remember that. Ray Charles was singing: if he was blind, I was sick. When we got back I ran upstairs, gave the sweets to my cousins and wondered what convent I should join, while downstairs my aunt tried to carry on a normal conversation while dreading what she would find out about the adventure. Never had there been such consternation about such a harmless gesture. I haven't seen him since 1964. I suppose I'll bump into him next week.

Michael Colgan
Truly, Madly, Deeply

I'm not sure how old I was, but the effect was devastating. Of course, I wish it could transpire that the film which caused such a reaction was now a classic or noted for its great acting, but sadly, nothing could be further from the truth. The star was Tommy Steele, the story could only have been mindless, it was called *The Duke Wore Jeans*, and I'm certain that the acting was abysmal; but it didn't matter, because I had fallen truly, madly, deeply in love with the leading lady. I first went with my pals. Said nothing. Then went back on my own. I've never forgotten her and I've never had the courage to find the film again.

Nuala O'Faolain

My memories are not of the art form of film, but of cinemas themselves. My memories are of courting. I and my contemporaries would have killed to get to the pictures, and we created dreadful scenes in our homes so that we wouldn't be one moment late going up the town to that magic building. But we were hormone-driven, not critique-driven. Our aim was to see and sense and parade past members of the opposite sex. And then to end up beside each other, in the warm, anonymous dark.

Lots of people my age have seen the opening credits of some of the most popular films of our time, and then the closing credits. And that's all. I remember the credits of *Rock Around the Clock*. I remember the credits of *The Misfits*. Of *Look Back in Anger*, where I actually sat upright for a while to admire Richard Burton. The Balbriggan cinema, and then the cinema in Fairview in Dublin, were the main venues for the burrowings of my teen years. On St Stephen's Day it was cinemas in O'Connell Street, when at last we escaped from our homes and the family Christmas to eye up our peers again.

No one had flats then. Even our parents didn't have cars. And unsupervised parties were as rare as hen's teeth. Cinemas were the one place where young people had an excuse to be together in privacy. I love them still, and still respond to the moment when the lights go down. But as to films themselves – I know hardly anything about them.

FEAR IN THE DARK

Luke Dodd

Visits to the cinema were very rare when I was a young child; the twice-daily routine of milking cows made any kind of day excursion difficult. Maybe as a child of the 70s, I found television a more available medium; and living in County Sligo, close to the border, we had access to the BBC and ITV. I can still recall the plot of every episode of Star Trek!

My earliest cinematic experience was *Mary Poppins*. At the time, I had not yet started school. One image from the film haunted me for years. Early on in the film, Mary Poppins uses her special powers to tidy the children's bedroom, and in the process the drawers of a chest continue to open and close feverishly. For some reason, I found this image truly frightening. Another memory of that day is of being fooled by the darkness of the cinema into thinking that it was night – only to emerge into daylight outside.

When I was at secondary school in Boyle, a 16mm projector was occasionally set up in the science lab. My uncle, the headmaster, had a great liking for Laurel and Hardy – a liking which I inherited and still have to this day. Stan Laurel said little but some of his lines were truly existential in scope: `You can take a horse to water, but a pencil has to be lead.'

When films like *Ben Hur* and *The Ten Commandments* came to town, special matinées were organised for the entire school. While I can't remember a single frame from any one of these films, I can well remember the excitement of getting time off from the dreary daily routine.

In college, I was a member of the Film Society. The programme was always stacked with a few worthy films which we, as students, felt should be seen whether or not they were enjoyable (Fellini comes to mind). Maybe it is impossible to re-create the magic of cinema in a lecture theatre. One projector, whirring away, spoils the seamlessness of reel changes.

The first film which really shocked me (in a good sense) was *Maeve* by Pat Murphy. It was showing at the Irish Film Theatre on Stephen's Green. I went with a Swiss friend, and we both emerged reeling from the cinema.

Maeve was an intelligent film by a young Irish director – a film as visually literate as it was politically complex. I suppose that the experience of this film coincided with a time in my life when I was beginning to think about things seriously.

At Strokestown, where I have lived for the the past ten years, visits to the cinema have been few and far between, as there is no cinema here. Maybe this has made the good visits more memorable. Still, I don't think that I will ever lose the sense of excitement I feel as the lights are dimmed, just before the film starts – no matter how many times I go. It's like a drug taking over your body.

Liz McManus

W_{hen} I was a child my family lived in various houses in Ireland and abroad. During that time a trip to the pictures on a Saturday afternoon had a certain ritualistic regularity. I saw *Bambi* in a cinema in The Hague and it gave me nightmares. History repeated itself years later in Stillorgan when my second son, at the age of five, shot out of the cinema in terror at the same film.

Adolescence was not an exciting time, filmwise or any other wise. Saturday trips to the Stella in Mount Merrion were dominated by the B films to the main feature. Detectives in trench coats. Impeccable BBC vowels. Pipe-sucking gentleman who couldn't act to save their lives.

When films got exciting was when we stopped going with the family and started going with boys. SEE YOU INSIDE. BACK ROW. No E-popping, rave-bopping teenager could experience a thrill equivalent to the one we felt when waiting in the queue at the Pavilion or the Adelphi in Dun Laoghaire. It was pure sex – which was more than you could say about what went on on-screen. That was the time of cowboy films where men were men, Indians were savages and women were idiots; or films set in desert oases populated by sultans who were into makeup and white slavery; or Doris Day and Rock Hudson. Then we all got sophisticated and there were great films. *The Pawnbroker, In the Heat of the Night, On the Waterfront* – 'I could have been a contender...'

But, looking back, one film stands out. I am eleven years old. The scene is Caherdaniel, County Kerry. The time is the late 50s, the days of oil lamps and gas lights. The film is *The African Queen*, introduced to the village by some enterprising operator. The parish hall is overflowing with people sitting on chairs, benches, and orange boxes. Katherine Hepburn looks wonderful. Humphrey Bogart looks hard-bitten and manly. And the generator is going thump, thump, thump in our ears so we can't hear a word they're saying. But we love every minute of it. That's the magic of cinema.

Albert Kelly
The Night of the Hearse

We have more fun with *The Rocky Horror Show* than any other picture. The only time we drop it is when we drop the later shows at Easter and Christmas. I'm only sorry that we don't have a visitors' book, because we've had loads of celebrities come in over the years.

One of the best nights we had was 'the Night of the Hearse'. It was exactly twelve o'clock, right on midnight. There should have been a bell tolling. And along came a hearse outside – no arrangement or anything – and there was a mourning coach behind. And eleven guys in evening dress got out and took the coffin out of the hearse. So I said to the staff, 'Open up all the doors, this could be a bit of fun!' So they very, very slowly put the coffin on their shoulders and walked in through the doors. They never spoke. They walked right down the aisle. We'd already stopped the film and put on the lights and the whole crowd was watching open-mouthed. They put the coffin down and a guy, also dressed in evening dress, got out. He bowed to the left audience, he bowed to the right audience and he bowed straight ahead. Then he got back into the coffin, they lifted it up and they walked out very slowly.

There was an extra guy, the eleventh man, and as they put the coffin back in the hearse, he wrote a cheque out to the cashier. I spoke to the guy as he left and asked him what it was all about.

'He's getting married tomorrow – this is his stag night.'

Michael Garvey

I remember the fright, not the film. Four years old and in something close to panic, I ploughed through an entire row of unsuspecting unaffected cinema-goers, pursued by my mother and my aunt, who was dragging my sister – younger than I and completely uninterested. No one in my family can remember the film – just the scene, one of the great clichés of cinema: a cattle stampede. My recollection, which haunts me to this day, was not of cattle passing me by to the left or the right but of the entire herd directing itself straight at me. (I was born in America and saw this film there: when I first came to Ireland I couldn't believe how hard it was to get cattle to move, never mind gallop.) I'm convinced that my initial shock over the stampede had to do with the speed and direction of the cattle, because the next film I remember seeing was *Bringing Up Baby* with Cary Grant, Katherine Hepburn and a leopard – animals again, and this time a wild and dangerous one featured in practically every shot; yet I never became anxious. In *Bringing Up Baby* neither the actors nor the leopard made direct contact with the audience by gaze or action. The audience remained spectators.

Today, film after film sets its sights directly on its audience. As we grow more laid-back and inured to shocks and surprises, film-makers pride themselves on their ingenuity in inventing bigger and newer frights. Sitting in our cinema seats, we can't stay stunned forever.

Feargal Quinn

My eighth birthday, the De Luxe in Dublin's Camden Street. The film: *The Princess and the Pirate* starring Bob Hope. We were not a regular cinema-going family, so 'the pictures' was a big event. For my father, mother and sister, this was going to be a fun movie, but to me it turned out to be a horror movie of the worst kind.

My memory is very clear, even after more than forty-five years. The hero (Hope) was in a bath house with the baddies. Tattooed on his chest was a map of where the pirate treasure was buried. Every time his chest emerged above the water he was in danger of having the map seen by the pirate chief!

Everyone else in the cinema may have thought this bobbing up and down in the water was fun, but for this eight-year-old, it was the most frightening terror that could happen to anyone. I insisted on leaving the cinema.

We never saw the end of this film. My sister didn't speak to me for days and I'll never find out now whether Bob Hope was discovered with the maps tattooed on his chest. But since he's still alive and well, playing golf in California, he must have escaped intact.

Frank McGuinness
St Mary's Hall

It is very dark in cinemas. St
Mary's Hall was no exception. I went
To the toilet. They are waiting. A gang.

I loved the cowboys and the indians.
This day I really was the Lone Ranger,
A masked man. They kicked the shit out of me,

I was that marked man. I did not know it then
I wore the mark-mask. It took twenty years
To remove the darkness from my two eyes

And see the light. They're still waiting, the gang.
Their feet, their fists, their spit. Down in Dublin
I found courage to go back to the pictures,

But still St Mary's Hall is in darkness.
Yes, it is very dark in cinemas.

X-RATED

Seamus Hosey
The Cold Hand of the Censor

When I was growing up on a farm in Co. Laois in the 1950s, there was a definite sense abroad that the forbidding concrete bulk of the cinema in Abbeyleix was the doubtful preserve of townies. However, the odd country lad, like my classmate Paddy Carroll in the National School, penetrated even the inner sanctum of the projection room where he helped out at weekends and displayed the occasional stolen strip of celluloid or black-and-white movie still, like treasures from an exotic world that was outside my experience.

My grandmother, who ruled the roost in our house, regarded the cinema with a certain amount of suspicion as an agent of moral corruption, unless the film showing had a healthy Irish theme (Jimmy O' Dea as King Brian of the Leprechauns in glorious technicolour in *Darby O'Gill and the Little People*) or, better still, combined national and religious icons in an edifying spectacle (Siobhan McKenna as the Virgin Mary in *King of Kings*). My father took me to the odd film that was of Irish and historical interest, in a kind of political pilgrimage to educate me about our troubled past. Such a film was *Shake Hands with the Devil*, which portrayed the stirring saga of Kerry O'Shea, an Irish-American medical student caught up in the War of Independence. The political complexities and nationalistic import of the struggle for Irish freedom were largely lost on my nine-year-old consciousness as the action blurred into a confusing maze of guns in coffins, Black and Tans raiding a pub, a spirited old Lady Fitzhugh (Sybil Thorndyke) dramatically embarking on a hunger strike, and a memorable closing image of a remorseful Kerry O'Shea throwing his gun away on the seashore after shooting his former IRA buddy.

It was not until I went to boarding school at Knockbeg College in 1963 that film became a regular part of my life. Every Sunday night the Study Hall was transformed into a makeshift cinema where the old and cumbersome whirring projector operated by one of the priests transported us magically to the dusty streets of the Wild West in *Gunfight at the OK*

Corral (with interruptions only to change reels) or *Down Three Dark Streets* with Broderick Crawford as a stocky FBI agent battling the forces of evil.

The sight of the big brown box holding the Sunday film caused a frisson of anticipation as it lay outside the priest-projectionist's room. You could read the film title from the label on the box, and I remember speculation was rife as to whether *A Town Like Alice* was really about the red-light district of an Australian mining town, as some of the smart boys had it; or, equally outrageous, whether *The Leather Saint* was about the canonisation of an Irish Christian Brother for his dedicated prowess with the strap.

The Sunday night film was invariably viewed in advance by Father Lennon or Father Noonan to censor any scenes likely to excite adolescent sexual fantasies or lead to unquiet dreams in the dormitory. On one occasion Homer nodded and in the middle of the packed Sunday night Study Hall, the cold hand of the censor was raised, literally. The film was a fairly harmless British bank robbery thriller called *On Friday At Eleven*, which moved from gangsters plotting in smoky rooms to a spectacular high-street heist and then the getaway. The scene moved to the coast of England, where the gang leader and his moll were lying low after the loot was divided out. The couple, after swimming in the sea, lie out in a secluded cove and begin to make love. Just as the brazen hussy's bikini-top was slipping from her shoulders, Father Projectionist leaped to his feet and placed a large hand in front of the lens, blotting out the offending scene, to a chorus of boos from the entire Study Hall.

Thus was adolescent virtue preserved, but adult curiosity was roused as to the unthinkable and maybe unlimited possibilities of cinema which were as yet undiscovered. The years since have been an exciting voyage of discovery where, so often, sitting alone in the darkened auditorium with ghosts and phantoms flickering on the silver screen, the world outside has been memorably illuminated and unforgettably enriched.

Brian D'Arcy

Going to the pictures was, and is, one of my favourite pastimes. As a small child growing up in rural Fermanagh, 'going to the pictures' meant putting on my hornpipe shoes, my white ankle socks, my First Communion suit and my plastic tie with the elastic loop tucked under my shirt. It meant walking half a mile to the bus stop and getting the number 58 bus which went from Derrylin to Enniskillen. It meant being taken by my mother, God be good to her, to the Regal Cinema in Enniskillen and watching anything from *The Song of Bernadette* to the Three Stooges.

It was a good cinema and the projector rarely broke down. I had been taught at school, primary and secondary, that if anything came up on the screen which placed exciting thoughts in my head, I should close my eyes until the scene was over and say three Hail Marys for purity. And with my mother alongside me, that's exactly what I did.

Not that there was much of it. Abbot and Costello, the Marx Brothers, Old Mother Reilly and anything with cowboys and Indians in it is not exactly steamy stuff.

What did affect me greatly, though, was the change-over from black and white to colour. That was special. We talked about it on the school bus, discussed it during Mass when the sermon was dull, and fought about it at half-time in football matches. After that, it seemed as if the world knew no bounds.

A little later, when I was eight, I was sent off to Omagh School. Bringing my sixpenny piece down to Miller's Cinema in the centre of Omagh, I was able to watch 'pictures' on my own. I felt like a grown man. I could discuss Mario Lanza and the music in *High Society*. That was maturity – and truth to tell, I didn't close both eyes every time something sexy came up on the screen. Many's a night I risked at least one eye.

Looking back, one of the disappointments in life is that films which seemed great and funny when I was young now seem ordinary. One such was a film called *Pardners* with Jerry Lewis and Dean Martin. My brother and I went to it on a Christmas Eve in Enniskillen. Almost every other young fellow in our county was at it as well. It was absolutely hilarious – or at least it was back then. If you were to ask me what was funny about it now, I couldn't tell you a single thing. However, anything Jerry Lewis did always seemed funny to me – I laughed for weeks at *The Nutty Professor*.

Next day at early Christmas Mass, at the most inappropriate time of the Mass, all of us thought of the funny bits of the film and started laughing. We made a disgrace of ourselves, our family and the parish. The priest turned round and hit each of us a good slap on the ear, but that was nothing to the slaps I got from my mother and father when I went home. Jerry Lewis and Dean Martin have a lot to answer for.

Years later, a film nearly cost me my vocation to the priesthood. During my days as a student in Mount Argus in Dublin, the system was so dreary, so foolish and so out of touch with reality that there were times when I had to escape from it to keep my sanity.

One day during study I quietly dressed, got my bicycle and cycled into O'Connell Street, locking the bicycle on the island there. In those days we had no clothes except our clerical ones. So here was this young student in heavy disguise, wearing a hat, a Roman collar and a black suit and coat, and feeling like a parish priest at eighteen years of age.

I had just about the price of the pictures in my pocket. And I went to see Frank Sinatra, another lifetime hero, in *From Here To Eternity* in the Capitol cinema on Prince's Street. Like its neighbour the Metropole, it's no longer in existence. But the Capitol cinema was an astonishingly beautiful theatre. It was at least as beautiful as the Gaiety is now. There were live shows in it but mainly it was a cinema.

I paid my money and slipped in the back. Had I been found out I would have been sent home instantly. When I settled in my seat my eyes got used to the darkness. And there sitting beside me was the Superior of the monastery, my boss. I nearly died. I waited until the next person came in and I got out.

But having paid my money, I wasn't going home. So I slipped into a seat in the back row where I could keep an eye on him and on the film at the same time. I cycled home that evening without having seen the end of the film. And all the way up Clanbrazil Street, I was composing a letter to my parents at home. I was thinking of an honourable excuse to explain my dismissal.

As it turned out, nothing happened. The next time I saw my boss was when we both went to the Choir to pray, as we all did then, at 2:00 in the morning.

Doing stupid things like that at eighteen years of age surely has the makings of a good film in it. Maybe someday when that Superior dies.

Richard Kearney
Extract from *Sam's Fall*

When it came to film, I found my place in the sun. I was elected auditor of the school's Film Society, set up by Br. Cilian in fifth class. We saw several New Wave films that first season, recommended by Cilian from his time in Paris – Resnais, Bresson, Fellini, Truffaut, Visconti, Godard. We even got to see some of the first American colour classics in the second term. Elia Kazan's *East of Eden*, Jack's favourite, with the shot of

Adam kissing his girlfriend in the barn full of melting ice cubes as the jealous brother Cal (James Dean) looks on; and Hitchcock's *Vertigo*, my favourite, where the retired cop Ferguson (Jimmy Stewart) is hired by his best friend to spy on his mystery wife (Kim Novak). I was puzzled by the fact that Ferguson had two names, Johnny and Scottie. And the mystery wife had three – Madeleine, Judy and Carlotta. I saw it several times while we had it on hire, relishing and reliving each scene. The opening frames of Ferguson's nightmare – head spiralling down through empty air off a steep roof. The bit where Carlotta Valdes leaps into San Francisco Bay only to be saved by Scottie who takes her home and changes her black and white clothes for a scarlet polka-dot gown. (Kim Novak looked the image of Aunt Madeleine in that scene.) The shots where Scottie takes Carlotta to a clothes shop and makes her dress up like the 'real' Carlotta. And the last sequence where he drives her to the old Spanish Mission to discover who she is... dragging her through the white-washed cloisters with her grey-green dress and dyed blond hair pinned back in a spiral curl, up the winding wooden steps and out on to the balcony where the crime is re-enacted again – and the victim falls to her death.

Having seen it several times, I knew most of the lines by heart, reciting them out loud to Jack and the others in a fake American drawl. I got the Jimmy Stewart almost perfect... though my Kim Novak was always a little hoarse...

Cilian's own favourite film was *L'Age d'Or*. And it proved in a curious way to be his fall from grace. *L'Age d'Or* was one of Buñuel's earliest black-and-whites, with English subtitles. We'd ordered it for the gala mid-term showing and sat, boys and monks alike, in the big hall, wide-eyed before those flickering grainy images: bishops chanting blessings for invading armies, a monstrance exiting from a taxi, maids running screaming from a blazing kitchen, a gardener shooting his own son dead, tumbrils driven through crowded salons, and the final sequences of Christ himself emerging like a criminal from an all-night orgy.

Dom Basil protested vigorously after the showing. The film, he insisted, was an assault on the Catholic Church. He remonstrated openly with Cilian for permitting such material to be shown to impressionable boys. Cilian might have said nothing, and that would have been that; but he replied, upping the ante, claiming education was first and foremost about seeing the other's point of view, and that if Christianity couldn't understand Buñuel's atheism it could understand nothing! Basil was enraged and, next day, circulated a three-page stenographed paper to all pupils as we filed into the refectory. Entitled 'Pornography, Art and Religion', it berated Buñuel as a cynical corrupter of morals. By the end of the following meal, Cilian was back on the attack, surrounded by a halo of cigarette smoke, distributing a Reply: 'Still an Atheist, Thank God – A Note on Luis Buñuel', in which he argued that Buñuel's surrealist film was an attack not on religion itself but on the temptation to make the Church into a second Tower of Babel, the idol of a second *age d'or*.

Marina Hughes
The Final Cut

I grew up in Kilmactranny in Co. Sligo. One of my earliest memories of film is of a family holiday in Galway when we were taken to see a film called *Where's the Tiger*. I must have been about three years old and it was probably the first film I saw. I was excited by the dark and these larger-than-life images. At the same time, an advertisement for Esso petrol was running with the catchy slogan 'Put a tiger in your tank!' and in my childish logic I associated the tiger of the film with the tiger of the ad. For some while afterwards, film became associated with pink paraffin in my child's view of the world.

The second outing to the cinema was to see *The Sound of Music* – this time in Dublin. My mother, who loves music, had explained that Julie Andrews was starring as Maria, so I was very fed up when the Dublin kids began pointing at the screen and shouting: 'There's Mary Poppins! There's Mary Poppins!' I knew better! Even at this early stage, though, my taste was beginning to take shape – best illustrated by yet another family outing, this time to Ballaghadereen, along with a seemingly endless number of boy cousins. The film was *Bandolero*, which I detested – although the boys, of course, loved it. I've never quite liked Westerns since.

Later on, when I was at boarding-school in the Ursuline Convent in Sligo, the nuns organised a screening every second Saturday evening. We saw the series of *Gigi* films, lots of Audrey Hepburn, and every conceivable version of *Wuthering Heights*. I'm not sure how the nuns selected the titles for our 'Saturday night at the movies' event, but evidently the process went a little awry on one specific occasion. It all started in our English class when we'd all purchased our brand new dictionaries – *The New Etymological Dictionary* – and marched into class displaying them. The word 'etymological' was quite a long one for us and our teacher diligently explained it in great detail and cautioned against confusing it with the similar-sounding word 'entomological'. She carefully pointed out the distinctions in meaning. 'Etymology is the study of words,' she said, 'while entomology is the study of insects, butterflies, and so on.' As an additional example, she referred to the forthcoming Saturday night's entertainment. She urged us to go and see the film as it was about collecting butterflies, and told us that we'd never forget the difference between etymology and entomology...

Well, the film was *The Collector*. We were all sitting there and when the film rolled, we thought 'Umm, this is interesting'. The sixth-years were thinking, 'What a change in policy – this is cool!' But the nuns were all sitting in the front row, and suddenly the screen cut to black – a nun had ripped off her veil and thrown it over the projector – which finished the entertainment for that evening.

HOME MOVIES

Shane Connaughton
The Majestic, Our Kitchen and the Luxor

The Majestic cinema was up at the other end of the town. We were not allowed to go in there at night. It was a palace of sin. It cost too much money. My friends went there. I looked at the posters stuck up outside. War, blood... women, beauty... Then I made my first Holy Communion. I was seven. I had reached the age of reason. My mother persuaded my father to let me go with my friends to see *Paleface* with Bob Hope and Jane 'Calamity' Russell.

One warm dark evening, Mattie Kennedy holding one hand, Brian 'the butcher' Smith the other, I was marched up the town and into the perfumed paradise of pleasure and escape. The jackass antics of Bob Hope eventually got the better of a town drunk who sat behind us singing 'Roll me over in the clover, let me down and do it again'.

On the way home the older lads referred to Jane Russell's 'big foot-balls'. I afterwards learned the proper name was 'bosom'. I was terrified by the Red Indians. 'I'd hate to get friggin' scalped, lads.' Mattie assured me there was no chance of that happening in Kingscourt. 'Only the Redskins have axes sharp enough.'

I never saw the inside of a cinema again until I was fourteen. We moved to a village at the other end of the county. Every Christmas, Superintendent Murray of the Garda Síochána came to the barracks and set up an 8mm projector in our kitchen. All the policemen's children crowded in, and with cake in one hand and lemonade in the other we watched Charlie Chaplin dance out of our wallpaper. In the dark I couldn't see the old furniture, the sewing machine, the lino. Just the glow of turf in the range and the white light burning in the projector and the cone-beam of magic sticking images to the wall. Charlie knew how to trick his enemies. Especially the cops. The real policemen in the kitchen laughed loudest when he did so... Our kitchen was a cinema! Fantastic...

I went from the village school to St Tiernach's in Clones. In Fermanagh Street was the best-named cinema in Ireland – or anywhere: the Luxor.

It sounded luxurious. Perfumed. Sexy. It was all that and more. John Maguire, Liam McElhinney, John Matthews, Gus Lennon – they brought their homework, did it on their laps, finished just in time for the big picture. It's the only way to do homework.

During the summer months, my brother Brian and I helped a local farmer named Richard McManus. As a reward he brought us to the Luxor. He introduced me to Marilyn. And then to Grace... In the warm, dark Luxor you could dream while you were awake! Those lips. Those arms. Those footballs... In his own kitchen Richard danced like Gene Kelly, drew a gun faster than John Wayne. And making hay was so much better when you had Marilyn walking beside you in the field. Or Grace – when I wasn't angry with her for marrying that Chaplinesque fella from the south of France.

Father Gallagher, one of our teachers, was furious with the name of the cinema. 'It should have been an Irish name.' The Pearse? The Barry? The Brian Boru? No, nothing could match the Luxor. The banks of the Nile lifted onto the banks of the Finn. The Valley of the Kings transported to Fermanagh Street. The old myths holding out the new. Egypt – Hollywood.

The Majestic is now a supermarket, the Luxor a broken empty building. I pass it every year on the way to the Ulster Final... As I pass I glance up. No Marilyn, no Grace... Still... I still have a kitchen. Where the dream ends and reality begins.

Liam Wylie

Joe Comerford's *Down the Corner* was the film that made the biggest impression on me. I saw it not at a cinema but at school. A 16mm projector was brought into our classroom to bring us a story of young fellows who looked and sounded like the watching audience.

This audience of ten- and eleven-year-old boys was used to James Bond movies, Westerns, war films and swashbuckling period pieces. Yet here was a film that took us not to these distant lands of adventure but to our own neighbourhood.

Micko Lynch, Buller and Pedro ambled along streets like ours. They were messing in a school cloakroom which looked like ours. Their teacher was a culchie like ours. Most of all, though, they spoke and dressed just like us.

Looking back, what must have amazed me most about *Down the Corner* was that my world could appear on a cinema screen. In 1976 I would not have been aware of the debates about 'realism' which surrounded *Down the Corner*. That day in fifth class we thought the film was gear!

Cyril Cusack
Knocknagow

This may have all or nothing to do with memories of childhood cinema, since it's principally about a film in which I was actually involved as far back as 1916 or 1917. I was six years of age and our touring company was playing Clonmel on a countrywide circuit tour, calling forth sobs and tears from our country audiences with a presentation of *East Lynne*, my mother as Lady Isabel, myself as Little Willie. At the time there would have been at least twenty companies on the road, including Ira Allen's Company of Irish Players; the Irish Theatre and National Stage Company with *The West's Awake*; Chalmer's; Dobell's; Mark Wynn's; and many others. (The Abbey Theatre was just then struggling into being amidst this profligacy of blood-and-thunder melodrama.) Not too far from Clonmel was Mullinahone, a village where a film based on Charles J. Kickham's *Knocknagow* was being shot. So we were all readily available to star.

I have some recollections of my mother making me up in the little market place of Mullinahone. In particular I recall the sharp prickle of the silver paper that bound the stick of Leichner No. 5 (which made us all look yellow) and the overpowering smother of powder from the puff my mother used.

Kickham's novel (the title means 'The Hill of the Smithy') embraces – if, indeed, you could call it an embrace – evictions, and the police with a battering-ram hammering at our cottage door, and our poor little cottage being set on fire. After the eviction of the O'Brien family (including myself) from the burning cottage, Father O'Brien (George Larchet, brother to Jack Larchet, maitre d'orchestre of the Abbey Theatre) went staggering along the country road, with child Cusack trailing behind, only to collapse on the grassy wayside. I remember it well because, with big holes in the corduroys I was wearing, I sat on a bunch of nettles.

However, I had already developed a certain professional sense and I did not stir away from the nettle stings.

At that point a lovely lady came down a sloping path from the Big House with a tray holding a jug of buttermilk and some homemade bread which I was called upon to gobble up as if I were starving. I was a fat little fellow and at no point of starvation. The lovely lady, I remember, was dressed in frilly white and the sunlight was glistening in every bubble topping the buttermilk – it was the first time I ever tasted buttermilk, and I have liked it ever since.

Finally, there was an episode in the film-story which I rather liked and in which I rather fancied myself. In this particular scene I get up and steal up the path to the Big House, pluck a rose from the roses round the door and, bubbling over with gratitude, kiss it, and return to my former prostrate position.

Needless to say, this episode was cut.

FLASHBACK

Tim Lehane
A-Z of my Cinema (1947 – 1961)

A for Atmosphere
That atmosphere when the lights went down, the speakers crackled into life, the smoke-filled projector beam... It was magic!

B for Bicycle
Bicycle? – Yes, how could you get to the Pavilion in Charleville if you hadn't a bike to cycle the six long, lonely miles of country road?

C for Courting
Courting in the back row wasn't the norm in rural cinemas. Maybe I was too busy looking at the screen! The first time I experienced it – I mean saw it, of course – was in Dublin in 1960.

D for Draw
As in the Wild West: 'Draw!'

E for Elephant
If the elephants were so smart how come Tarzan had to shout at the top of his voice for them to come and help?

F for Fantasy
That wonderful fantasy, as you cycled home, that you were the hero – that an adventure was just around the corner...

G for Great
As in 'That was great!' The other word you needed to be a film critic was 'useless'.

H for High
In *High Noon*, sheriff Will Kane takes a sheet of paper and begins to write 'The last will and testament of...' as the clock ticks relentlessly, and the theme song goes, 'Do not forsake me, oh my darling...'

I for Indian
And you've guessed it – the Indians were always the bad guys then.

J for Jungle
Green Hell was the first jungle film I saw. I was four. I'm still in shock!

K for Kiss
'Oh no!' – Get on with the adventure.

L for Laurel
And who could forget Hardy? I'm going to take an action against their estate. They made me laugh so much it hurt.

M for Marx Brothers
'Is this anarchy?' 'Whaddayamean another key?'

N for National Anthem
THE END. NATIONAL ANTHEM. ALL STAND.

O for Outlaw
I feel another stage-coach coming on.

P for Plague
And for panic, as in *Panic in the Streets*. Can they find the plague-carrier (Jack Palance)? That was scary.

Q for Queue
I couldn't believe my eyes – a queue stretching at least a quarter of a mile outside the Theatre Royal for *Twist around the Clock* (1961).

R for Robin
And his merry trees and men of oak. You know the idyll.

S for Sissy
A soppy story about an Austrian princess. I'd just had a tooth extracted. 'You have to come with me or I won't be allowed go... please, please, please...' pleaded my sister. I went. Ouch!

T for Thank
'Thank you very much ladies and gentlemen for your kind attendance here tonight. Next week we'll have a thrilling Tarzan adventure. During the interval we'll have a raffle: tickets tuppence each, four for sixpence.' That was the weekly speech in the old school hall in the village.

U for Undress
Nobody much in a state of except Tarzan – but that was okay – it was a real jungle out there.

V for Vulture
Oh no! not another wagon train ambushed?

W for Wayne
Wagon. West. War-paint. Wilderness. Whoops. Walk...

X for X-rated
'Hey, this is London. It's 1960. I'm eighteen.'

Y for You
'You dirty, lyin' skunk.' 'You rotten, two-faced...' etc. etc. etc.

Z for Zink
'Vot do you zink you are doing, you fool?' How did we recognise the foreigners?

John Kavanagh

I've always been fascinated by film. When I was a kid I had a hand-cranked film projector, an old thing called a Piccolo, that screened 9.5mm films with a sprocket down the centre. I also acquired lots of films. You used to buy them in a chemist's shop and I remember that they were very expensive – fifty feet of Tom Mix or something was a couple of quid: no joke in the 50s. Then I'd have my own film shows: I'd bring kids into the house, put up a white sheet and show them films. It was the miracle of projection that fascinated me. In fact I wanted to be a film technician first of all. I was working in a processing film laboratory – Lyle Smith's, an agent for Agfa home film – when I joined the Brendan Smith Academy because I saw a prospectus that said that somebody from the Academy had ended up as some sort of technician. So I joined them and sort of fell into acting.

My first experience of film was in either the Dundrum Parish Hall or a convent. I'm not sure what the first film I saw was, but *The Song of Bernadette* was among the earlier ones. Subsequently I went to film shows in the Marian Hall to raise money for the building of the church and such like. The whole village, the whole community from the environs, would come to see these shows. There was just one 16mm projector, so you had to wait for the projectionist to change reels.

All the local cinemas I used to go to were known by their abbreviations (except the Odeon – it was always the Odeon). The Sandford in Ranelagh (now Wong's restaurant) became the Sanner. The Princess in Rathmines was the Prinner. It had a foyer like a loo – all the walls were tiled. Why, I have no idea. I always remember how in there at the Saturday matinées, you'd have the follier-upper, like a serial. In the Princess, they had two kids in the one seat, although you were charged the full price. You had twice the amount of people that should have been in the place. It was dreadful and the noise of the kids was absolutely deafening. It rarely settled down. The ushers were like ringmasters. You'd need cattle prods to keep some of the kids in check. They'd piss on the floor and the auditorium would be raked – they'd follow the trickle back up from the screen to the source. Dangerous times... And if there was a balcony, they'd be throwing things down on top of you, cigarette butts and stuff.

Years later, my first job was as a trainee cinema manager – in the Capitol cinema on Prince's Street, a wonderful cinema with a great restaurant. We had to wear dress suits every evening. The fact that I was a manager didn't detract from the magic of the place; it was wonderful to be there, standing in this huge emporium. I also worked in the Ambassador. I loved both. They were both very posh and both owned by Capitol and Allied theatres.

When I was there in the early 60s, James Stewart came to the cinema one day during Easter when the cinemas were closed for Holy Week – they did all the renovations then. He came in and the workmen were all on the ladders. They'd recently shown *The Man Who Shot Liberty Valance*, and one of the workmen said 'Don't go in there, Mr Stewart, Liberty Valance is waiting for you.' And James Stewart replied, 'He can't be – I shot him.'

I remember when *Ben Hur* came out at the Ambassador – I think it was 1958. At that time it took ages for films to get here, so the papers ran an application form for your tickets to the show and you nominated a date and time. I remember I booked about two months in advance to see this thing and I could only get the second row. I nearly went blind looking at *Ben Hur*, even having booked two months in advance. And I remember at the end of the film, the place was black, and I went out through this exit near the screen and ended up in the Rotunda Gardens, where I'd never been before. It turned out to be an emergency exit. It was very difficult to get out of the gardens once you got into them.

Billy Roche
in conversation about
memories of Wexford cinemas

There were three cinemas in Wexford – the Abbey, the Cinema Palace and the Capitol – and they were situated throughout the town. The Abbey was on my side, the Cinema Palace was right in the middle of the Main Street, and the Capitol was on the far end of the town. There was no sense of territoriality about the cinemas – people came to the cinemas from all over, depending on the film.

It was very good value, with two houses screening two films a night, and a change every two nights. And you could watch four screenings a night because nobody would put you out. The Scratch (the cheap part) was 4d, the middle part was 10d and the balcony would be 2/-. There was a distinct difference in the clientele in each of the sections. The messenger boys were in the Scratch, but it wasn't all romantic – there were dirty old men with chips, and a horrible smell in the toilets. We used to get the money to go to the tenpenny part, but we'd go to the Scratch so we'd have sixpence to spend on sweets. You felt kind of tough down among the messenger boys.

The balcony was occupied by older teenagers who were working and who would bring the girlfriend. A sixpenny ice cream, which was like a huge sandwich, was usually bought for the girlfriend. When my sister, Brenda, was brought on a date, she was regularly mortified because I used to shout up at her from the Scratch – just to annoy her. Later, as we got older and became interested in girls, we were ashamed to be seen in the Scratch, but we went anyway. We sneaked in when the lights went down and sneaked out before they came up, in case anyone saw us.

I remember one film which was heart-breaking – it was called *The Day They Gave Babies Away*. It's not a famous film but it really affected me. It was about a family of fourteen children whose mother and father had died, and the eldest brother was giving the children away at Christmas when there was snow on the ground. I remember going home that day and wallowing in the warmth of the kitchen at home, with the smell of a jam tart baking in the oven...

Small-town Irish men – in fact, small-town people around the world – feel embarrassed about talking about art, so in Wexford people summed up a film with 'That was a right film' or 'That was dirt'. I couldn't believe it when I asked one fellow about *Cool Hand Luke* and he said: 'Yes, it was a great film. He gets killed in the end' – which completely ruined the suspense. He didn't realise that it mattered.

There was a fellow who was called Cagney because he looked a bit like Jimmy Cagney. *Shake Hands with the Devil* was very big in Wexford. It was a very beautiful film and Cyril Cusack had a lovely cameo role as a pacifist IRA man. There's a nice scene of Cusack sitting smoking his pipe, with Cagney as the IRA man who wouldn't lie down. It has a certain echo today – with an American entering the scene, to boot.

When rock and roll came in, teenagers were born. I remember all the British films with people like Billy Furey, the Beatles, Cliff Richard. I was about twelve or thirteen and I'd heard of Elvis and I'd seen Bill Haley with his little kiss-curl, so I expected Elvis to look like Haley – who, to me, was an old man with a kiss curl. But when Elvis came on the screen, he was this beautiful creature – in jeans. I hoped that I looked like Elvis in my own jeans, and lots of us were going around imitating him and his swagger – just as we'd imitated the action in the Westerns, riding brushes up and down the street, duelling or playing out the story of the film with our toy soldiers at home.

I loved all the John Ford Westerns, especially *The Searchers*. Scorsese says that *Taxi Driver* is the story of *The Searchers* retold in an urban setting. It's an old theme – going into Hades and getting back alive. I clearly remember Tad Hunter playing the young guy, and the wonderful ruth-lessness of John Wayne's character. There were beautiful subtle moments – it's never said, just hinted, that he is a bank robber, or that he's attracted to his brother's wife. Nowadays, you'd see the two of them in bed. At that time, billowing curtains or waves washing upon the shore was enough.

I didn't see much theatre when I was growing up, so I learnt a lot from the pictures. Sharp, snappy dialogue – I loved wise-guy quips. One of my favourites was *Cool Hand Luke* – and my own film *Trojan Eddie* is a little nod to it. I love misfits and those who challenge authority. I can practically recite the entire dialogue of *Cool Hand Luke*. It's set up so deftly. When Luke is caught cutting the heads off parking-meters, he says:

'I was just passin' the time, Captain.'

And the Captain responds: 'Well, you got some time to pass now, boy. You got yourself three years here.'

Thaddeus O'Sullivan

There was nothing much to do when I was young. The other kids mostly played football and I hated sports, so I spent a lot of time at the pictures. I was allowed to go on my own very early. When I was eight I saw *Shane* at the Sandford Cinema in Ranelagh where we lived (it's a Chinese restaurant now). *Shane* was a film about a young boy who looked up to this gunfighter character and wanted his father to be like him. We liked it because it was about growing up, about feelings you had about your parents.

I liked horror films a lot, like *Dracula* and *Phantom of the Opera*. Anything we liked we saw over and over again. We'd try to see a film more times than anyone else. I remember one nutter on our street saw *Dracula* fifty times! He was our local vampire and was always jumping out from behind a bush and trying to stick his teeth into your neck.

The lone gunman type appealed to me – the kind that always dressed in black. He'd save the town from some awful fate and then just mysteriously ride off into a very uncertain future, leaving behind the girl who loved him. It was that bit I thought was peculiar. I knew I could never be the lone gunman because I could never have done that.

My father used to take me to the Princess very early on, sitting on the cross-bar of his bike.The Princess was a very old cinema in Rathmines and was pulled down in the 70s. He liked Westerns, so that's what I saw with him. One film I saw there had subtitles. I can't remember what it was – just that it was weird.

The Princess had a lot of double seats which were popular with couples in the evening. For the matinées, the usher wanted to pack the place, so he'd squeeze as many kids as he could into each row. We'd be sitting on top of one another, three or four to a double seat, hardly able to see the screen. Sometimes, if we had to queue in the rain beforehand, the place would be like a steam bath from the wet clothes, and the stuffy damp smell would be nearly unbearable. Sometimes I went to see my Cabra cousins and we'd go to the 'Bo' (the Bohemian in Phibsboro). But the crowd up there were a bit too wild for me, and being that far north of the Liffey was like being in a foreign country.

Later, when I was twelve or thirteen, visits to the pictures got a bit more interesting. It was like this: you got there early, grabbed a back seat and kept the one beside you free. The girl you fancied was probably giggling with her friends a few rows in front. Eventually you'd persuade her to come and sit beside you. Her friends were always the problem, though. The other problem was how to see the film at the same time. The girl could do that, because she'd just sit there looking straight ahead while you did all the work. You'd be full of passion and she'd be watching the film over your shoulder.

My week at the pictures was: Wednesday night at the Sandford, Saturday at the Sandford or the Stella in Rathmines, and Sunday matinée at the Kenilworth (now the Classic in Harold's Cross). That was always a riot. No one watched the film and there were always fights.

My ma went to the pictures too. She'd meet her sister every Wednesday under Clery's clock and they'd go to see a film. Years ago, audiences were allowed to sit through as many showings as they wanted. My mother and her sister usually went into a film when it was half over. When it finished they'd stay on to see the film again. They've been going to the pictures for fifty years and I reckon they've seen about 4,500 films, not one of them on video.

Eventually I discovered snooker and didn't see so many films. We had begged my da for years to get a television. He'd always said, 'A television is coming into this house over my dead body.' We got one in the end, but of course he was the only one who watched it.

Then I got interested in serious films – 'art' films, or whatever you want to call them. The Academy Cinema in Pearse Street was the only place you could see stuff like that. I saw Truffaut's first film there, *The 400 Blows*, and Fellini's *La Dolce Vita*. I saw films by Frenchmen Jacques Prévert (writer) and Marcel Carne (director) – *Les Enfants du Paradis* and *La Bête Humaine*, which starred my favourite actor of all time, Jean Gabin. I felt I was seeing real people on the screen for the first time; but even so, the films were magical. They appealed to my imagination in a way that American films never did (and still don't). Recently I met the cinematographer of those two films. Henry Alkan is eighty years of age now and still working. I wasn't surprised to discover that he's a friendly and sympathetic man, since I'm sure his personality lives on in those films.

Years before, there was another cinema in Pearse Street (I can't remember what it was called). On a school trip I saw *Mise Éire* and *Saoirse* there. These were documentaries about the 1916 Rising and the birth of the nation. But the part I remember best was Sean O'Riada's music score. It was tremendous – very epic, full of emotions and feelings. (I heard another great score like it years later: Morricone's music for *The Battle of Algiers*, also about an uprising). It felt strange to be watching and enjoying a film that was in Irish, because at that time we hated everything to do with the Irish language. It also seemed strange to be doing anything organised by our school that was interesting or useful. Westland Row CBS was a real dump. The brothers brought us to these films because Patrick Pearse had been to the school. God only knows what he learned there.

Gabriel Byrne
Reel Memories from *Pictures in My Head*

Looking back to an evening in the half-light of that room [at my grandmother's house], filled with the smell of lilac from her garden, among the faded photos and framed jigsaw puzzles, and stuffed owls, I know that memory has made all the evenings I spent there become as one. And I know that this was my first theatre, the beginning of my love for darkened rooms where words and image and music had power to move the soul in transports of delight, as the poet says. She loved talking and telling stories and books and music, but most of all my granny loved the pictures.

I remember crossing the park, my hand in her hand as she took me to the pictures for the first time. We stood for minutes watching the swans on Fairview Lake, but I was impatient to be away, for the thrill of the picture-house was greater than any swan. We waited for the doors to open, behind a sign on the pavement which said 'One shilling'. A man dressed in a red uniform came out and beckoned us and the other people to a glass box. Granny opened her purse and carefully counted out the coins, and received a ticket with a hole in it, which she gave to another man who stood like a soldier in front of two doors. He took the tickets and tore them and gave us back one half and kept the other and looped it onto a piece of string.

From inside the doors I could hear loud voices, but not like the voices of real people, and I started to feel afraid and she looked at me and smiled and took my hand tightly again and said, 'There's nothing to be afraid of. It's only the pictures.'

All around the foyer there were painted photographs of men with thin black moustaches and women with bright red lipstick like my mother. Then the sentry pulled back the door and we were in darkness with the noise of those strange voices all around us. We edged our way along by a wall like blind people, me holding on to her coat for fear, till suddenly, in an explosion of blinding colour, I saw before me the bluest sea I could ever imagine, and on it two huge boats with sails, sailing under a vast blueness of sky. I turned my head in terror into her body, and for an eternity of moments I dared not look again. When I opened my eyes I saw a light beam in the darkness and a voice asked for our tickets, as it came toward us. And with her arm around me, we followed the dancing light as it lit our way along the steps, 'til we found our seats and I sat down overwhelmed by the fear and the mystery and the magic of it all. But as the wonder grew, the terror died. And so I came to know the lovely dark womb of the picture-house for the first time.

Now the lights came slowly on from red stars of glass set high above us in the blue roof and around the walls from flickering lamps. And a snowy curtain that folded into silver trees as it slowly fell, covered the sea and the boat and the white writing and the voices.

'Was that a picture, granny?'

'No, that was only an old trailer,' she said. Then she gave me a marshmallow mouse and a Trigger bar which I broke in two over my knee. And she hoped I wouldn't be afraid of the next picture because the banshee was in it. But so was Jimmy O'Dea and he was great gas.

A girl in a yellow coat came up the steps between the seats with a tray of sweets. And we bought two Toblerones, and she kept one for after and we split the other between us.

And now the curtain of trees was going up to the roof again, and the lights faded 'til I could see only the outline of things. And then nothing at all. Then it began. The first picture I ever saw – *Darby O'Gill and the Little People.*

Time has dimmed the memory of the plot, but I remember the fairies and Jimmy O'Dea and the banshee, charging white and terrifying over the hill. And somebody throwing a lantern at the dreaded thing and as it burst into flames the gasps and screams of the few people who were in the audience. But above all I remember a smiling man and a girl sitting on the edge of a swaying haycart, talking as the music played. Nothing more. But the memory of those scenes has stayed with me always.

When we came out it was raining and the lights from the shops shone in the wet pavements but now I looked at everything as if for the first time. For I knew that something had been born within me. And that the world outside the picture-house would never be quite the same again. That evening she played the accordion as usual but the tune she played from under her fingers was the music from the picture. And as she sang,

Oh for the days of the Kerry dancing,
Oh for the call of the piper's tune,

I made of my winged chair a swaying haycart, and that night I slept dreaming of lanterns and silver stars and Jimmy O'Dea sailing the biggest of ships on the bluest of seas.

Michael Dwyer
Flashbacks

Going to the cinema for the first time: to see *The Barretts of Wimpole Street* at the Ambassador in Dublin when I was five. Almost two decades later, when I was twenty-three and an amateur actor with the Group Theatre in Tralee, I acted in the play of *The Barretts of Wimpole Street* – in the role of a very elderly gentleman.

From when I was five, going to the cinema with my parents three times a week, every week, in Tralee – and taking in double-bill matinées with my schoolfriends every Saturday and Sunday. The bug was biting deeply.

In my schooldays, my daily routine after class each and every afternoon, rain or shine, of touring around Tralee's three cinemas (or gaffs, as we called them) – the Ashe, the Picturedrome and the tacky Theatre Royal – to check out any new posters or stills in their front-of-house displays.

The sense of deprivation I felt when I went to boarding school in Killarney at fifteen and I was reduced to one movie a month – always something utterly innocuous chosen by the priests. To compensate, I went to Dublin for weekends on my own every holiday-time and crammed in virtually every movie in the city centre from 2 pm on Friday – with late-night shows on Friday and Saturday – to 5:30 pm on Sunday, when the last train left Heuston for Tralee.

Seeing the extraordinary, eye-opening *Bonnie and Clyde* for the first time when I was sixteen – and going to see it three more times in the same week.

At eighteen, seeing the foreign-language classics I previously had only read about, and discovering Bergman, Fellini et al. at the Film Society in Trinity College, Dublin.

In my early twenties, the buzz of programming the Tralee Film Society and filling the 630-seat former Ashe cinema on Monday nights through the winter/spring seasons with audiences who travelled from all over Kerry for alternative cinema. We couldn't afford a new screen, so we painted the back wall white – the clarity was so good that nobody noticed.

Around the same time, meeting a film director for the first time – the sublime François Truffaut, one of my all-time favourites – at the Cork Film Festival; and discovering that in person, Truffaut radiated all the warmth, charm and humanity of his movies.

Writing my first film review for *In Dublin* in 1979. The film was the negligible sequel *International Velvet*, but I spent hours on it.

The nervousness I felt before conducting my first big movie star interview – with Meryl Streep in London in 1980 – and how infectious and calming her serenity was.

The excitement of going to the Cannes Film Festival for the first time in 1982 and, like the proverbial child let loose in a sweet-shop, gorging myself on a wealth of international cinema for eleven days – and to top it all, the spine-tingling pleasure of seeing the world premiere of *ET* on the closing day. Now I'm a Cannes veteran, having attended the entire event for the past fifteen years in a row and spent thirty weeks of my life at this festival.

Founding the Dublin Film Festival with Myles Dungan in 1985 and seeing it become a reality – and a popular success – after just three wild and crazy months of preparation.

Attending the Irish premiere of *The Commitments* at the Savoy in Dublin in 1990 – the most audibly emotional screening I've ever experienced.

My ten favourite films – the list changes daily – in alphabetical order:
Barry Lyndon
Battleship Potemkin
Bonnie and Clyde
Citizen Kane
His Girl Friday
La Nuit Américaine (Day for Night)
Raging Bull
Three Colours: Red
The Wild Bunch
Z

Luke Gibbons
That Faraway Look

Leitrim has only one cinema left now, but in the 50s and 60s there were two a short distance from our village: the Roxy in Drumshanbo and the Gaiety in Carrick-on-Shannon. On Sunday afternoons, if there was no match on the radio, we'd head on our bikes for the matinée in the Roxy. It wasn't exactly a pleasure palace: the roof was made of the kind of red galvanized metal used for haysheds, and the steps to the balcony were on the outside, weathered by the rain. We never checked what film was on, but we cheered if it was a Western, and groaned if there was a female lead because the love scenes would get in the way of the action. Once Virginia Mayo's name came up on the credits, and someone in the back of the cinema shouted that Virginia is in Cavan, for God's sake. It was strange coming out into the daylight again when the film was over, adjusting our eyes like miners coming out of the coalmines in Arigna.

The Gaiety in Carrick was more of a night out. We'd go with our parents at the weekend, and it was best to book beforehand for seats on the balcony. Films brought out the faraway look in my mother's eyes, like when she listened to Paul Robeson or Mario Lanza. My father preferred comedies, especially the Marx Brothers; my favourite gag was when Harpo combed his hair in a mirror, and then turned it around in order to see the back of his head.

The banshee scene in *Darby O'Gill and the Little People* scared us so much that my father marched us up to the projection room afterwards, and, pointing to a big piece of machinery which seemed to have two bicycle wheels sticking out of it, said: 'Now, are you satisfied? It's only a film.'

A Night to Remember, about the sinking of the *Titanic*, also had a lot to answer for. A few weeks after seeing it, we went down to Cobh to meet an American aunt who was coming home on an ocean liner, and my young brother panicked out in the bay when he heard it was called the *Brittanic*. Nothing would convince him that it was not doomed. When we finally got on board, I remember writing out 3909 ON, and holding it up in front of a mirror to see if it really said NO POPE. That was the number the Protestants gave to the *Titanic* in the Belfast shipyards, so no wonder it sank.

The little I read about films came from the comic *Film Fun*, and, later, from the more heavy-duty *The Word* magazine. *Film Fun* carried story strips about real-life actors and actresses, but I'd hardly heard of any of them. When Shirley Eaton from the rival comic *Radio Fun* later cropped up in *Goldfinger*, however, I felt I had an inside track on her. I still had to admit that James Bond's gold Aston Martin was the main attraction, and I bought the Matchbox toy, complete with ejector seat, for my small brother, secretly wishing I could keep it myself.

Films were not always fun, though. Some were educational. The whole school was taken to see *The Ten Commandments*. I wrote to my aunt in America about it, hoping she might send me five dollars because of my grasp of such a serious film. *Mise Éire* was the other great state occasion, and it was unusual not only because of the Irish language but because there seemed to be no story in it; there were photographs and pages from newspapers instead. All the good was taken out of it when we were told we had to write an essay in Irish about it afterwards. I would have preferred to write about *Shake Hands with the Devil*, but the nearest I got to it was a review of it in *The Word* magazine, with a picture of Jimmy Cagney trying to save Ireland instead of de Valera.

The problem with the reviews in *The Word* was that you couldn't see the films for ages afterwards – unless, that is, you went to Dublin. *Ben Hur* was on in Dublin for so long that I thought it was the name of a cinema. When we eventually saw it, the teacher reminded us that Stephen Boyd was one of our own, even if he was from Northern Ireland,

and not to forget that when we saw the chariot race. The best thing in Dublin was the Funnies in Grafton Street, where they showed cartoons all day long. My parents used to leave us there while they had more important things to do, and we watched the same cartoons and newsreels to our heart's content, over and over again. This was when I first took an interest in soccer, watching Spurs beat Leicester City in the FA Cup on the Movietone News. Danny Blanchflower was captain, and he was also from Northern Ireland.

Films impinged directly on reality when my mother, on a visit to Dublin, tried to get a glimpse of Elizabeth Taylor and Richard Burton, who were staying at the Shelbourne during the filming of *The Spy who Came in from the Cold*. We went down to Smithfield where they had the set for Checkpoint Charlie, and it was hard to believe that the Berlin Wall and communism lay just beyond. It was also hard to believe that it was the same Elizabeth Taylor who I had had a sneaking regard for in *National Velvet*.

Films became part of my inner life when I went out with my first steady girlfriend. I loved the way she held my arm, blinded by the dark, when we entered the cinema, before getting used to each other again. The highlight during our first year was the Swedish sex-education film *Helga*, which for some reason got a general release in Ireland. An ambulance was parked outside the Gaiety every night to look after those who fainted during the childbirth scenes, and we left the cinema somehow feeling older. One film, however, had special meaning: *Splendour in the Grass* with Natalie Wood and Warren Beatty. Our hearts went out to the young couple when they were having difficulties in their relationship, and afterwards I remember we stopped to look at wedding photographs in Keaney's window, our reflections inside the darkened glass.

MAGIC LANTERNS

William Trevor
Nights at the Excel

My brother and I were given a cinematograph, an inexpensive toy that promised hours of wholesome winter fun. It came with off-cuts of films featuring Red Indians on horseback, and was lit by a tricky arrangement of torch battery and bulb. You darkened the room, turned a handle, and the Indians appeared on the wallpaper, waving tomahawks and chasing something that never came into the picture.

The conjunction between bulb and battery regularly failed, or the film jammed and tore, or the repetition of the Indians' pursuit of the unknown became tedious, even when the film was run backwards. So we scraped at both sides of the off-cuts with a penknife, ridding them of the galloping Indians and leaving us with transparent strips of celluloid. On these we inscribed with pen and ink a series of grimacing match-stick figures, which jerkily changed position on the wallpaper. Inspired, we added red ink to blue, and Technicolor came to our screen.

That was my first working association with the world of film, although I had long delighted in Gracie Fields marching the citizenry through the streets, and Jack Buchanan dancing his heart out, and a strange film in which a man was shot over the telephone. Going to the pictures was the best thing in the world: the smell of old cigarettes on a sunny afternoon, the curtainless screen, the scratchy music before there was the Western Electric Sound, the sleepy MGM lion, the searchlights of 20th Century Fox.

In 1940, in the town of Tipperary, the cinema went up in flames, taking with it Clark Gable and Norma Shearer in *Idiot's Delight*. But Mr Evans, a bicycle-shop proprietor, built a new one, with baskets of flowers suspended from the hugely jutting ledge that formed a roof above pale marble steps, and a motif of butterflies on curtains that marvelously changed colour several times before each programme began. Mr. Evans called his masterpiece the Excel. Forty-five years later I changed the name and changed Mr Evans as well, but if the novella I called *Nights at the*

Alexandra is dedicated to anyone it is that wartime entrepreneur and benefactor. For three nights in a row and twice on Saturdays Nelson Eddy sang in the beautiful Excel. James Cagney was the hero of the Fighting 69th there, Robert Donat and Rosalind Russell were married there. Edna May Oliver chased the donkeys from her green, Vivien Leigh sank into prostitution, Destry rode again. And yet to come were *They Died With Their Boots On* and *Random Harvest*, and the Yacht Club Boys in *Coconut Grove*.

Today, when earnest PhD students or media interviewers ask about influences, I say there are two: the detective stories and thrillers I read when I should have been reading such works as *The Cloister and the Hearth*, and the way in which films are made. Playing about with words on paper is not wholly unlike playing about with celluloid. You cut as a film editor cuts. As the narrative develops, your own first images have to go if they aren't the right ones any more. You change the order of scenes. You remove what has become clutter, as easily as you once scraped away Indians with feathered headgear. Not all fiction-writers operate in this manner; hardly any did in the past. But how films achieve their impact is something that now can be made use of, if you're that way inclined. You can splice your fiction, using scissors and glue.

There's a darker side to all of this, of course. Raiding the world of film may be a productive exercise for the fiction writer, but when the raiding is the other way round it's not nearly as agreeable an experience. Good novels do not always make good films, although there are impressive exceptions. To avoid disappointment, the wise novelist keeps his expectations in check, well aware that on its way to the cinema the novel becomes the film director's property. With this change of ownership, it may be squeezed where it shouldn't be squeezed, expanded where it shouldn't be expanded, smartened up with a bit of sleaze, made visually exciting when it should be shadowy, and have an upbeat ending tacked on.

There is also the question of 'input', a much-used word in the modern film industry. No matter how jealously the director may wish to guard what he feels is his alone, he cannot afford to ignore the insistence of those who share his project with him. There is, for instance, the understandable desire of the film's backers to make money out of what they have paid for. The scriptwriter has a few ideas. Suggestions come from the producer, whose eye is already on the Oscar ceremonies.

The characters in one of my own novels were given eagles' wings by a Hollywood scriptwriter. In another, a sperm bank – a kind of cashpoint, I remember – was introduced, and a band of Javanese dancers cheered up a Dublin suburb. Fortunately, neither enterprise was proceeded with,

Above: Cyril Cusack as a child actor in *Knocknagow* (from the Press Book 1918)

Below: Cover of the Press Book, *Knocknagow*, 1918

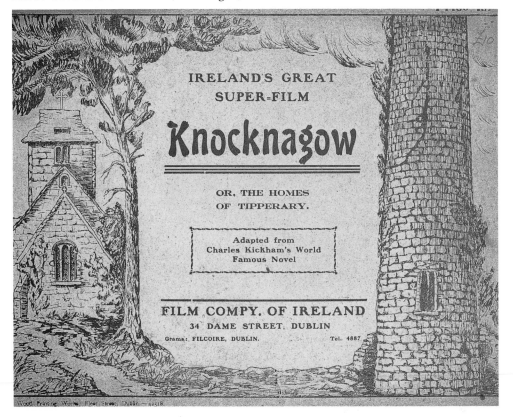

An *Volta*. Céad-Phictiúrlann na hÉireann.

Orange Maid

The 'drink-on-a-stick'

Great Star of the cinema
and biggest sales-winner
for years

*

Left: Book Mark
advertisement for
Orange Maid lolly,
The *Kinematograph
Year Book,* 1956

Left: Line-drawing of the Volta Cinema,
Mary Street, Dublin, Ireland's first cinema,
founded by James Joyce in 1909
Below: The Grand Cinema, Fairview, Dublin,
1955

Above: From the Disney film, *Darby O' Gill and the Little People*, 1959
Below: The State Cinema, Phibsboro, Dublin, 1956

Above: Queues outside the Strand Cinema, North Strand, Dublin
Below: Interior, Adelphi Cinema, Longford, *circa* 1959-60

Airplane positioned over the entrance to the Ambassador Cinema, Dublin
during the run of *The Blue Max*, 1966

KILTIMAGH (Co. MAYO).

SAVOY CINEMA (RCA).—Prop., Kiltimagh Cinema Co. 600 seats.

KINGSCOURT (Co. CAVAN).

MAJESTIC (RCA).—Prop. P. Macken. 450 seats.

KINSALE (Co. CORK).

PIER CINEMA.—Prop., J. Fitzgerald. 340 seats.

LETTERKENNY (DONEGAL). Pop. 2,308.

LA SCALA (WE).—Prop., A. C. Cinemas (Ireland), Ltd. 850 seats. Separate shows. Prices, 10d. and 1s. 8d. Booked at Londonderry. Station, Letterkenny.

LIFFORD (Co. DONEGAL). Pop. 490.

RITZ CINEMA (RCA).—Prop., Barry and Shortt, Ltd., Main Street, Lifford. Phone, 71. 350 seats. Two shows daily. Separate performances. Three or four changes weekly. Prices, 9d. to 2s. Booked at Drumbeny House, Lifford. CinemaScope. Station, Lifford.

LIMERICK (LIMERICK). Pop. 40,000.

CARLTON (WE). Phone, Limerick 61.—Prop., Carlton Cinema (Limerick), Ltd. Phone, 1086. 800 seats. Booked at Hall. Continuous from 2.30 p.m. Prices, 1s. to 2s. 6d. Two changes weekly. Screen, 35 ft. wide. Proscenium width, 35 ft. CinemaScope. Station, Limerick.

COLISEUM (WE). Phone, Limerick 259.—Station, Limerick, C.I.E. (Closed).

GRAND CENTRAL (WE). Bedford Row. Phone, Limerick 561.—Prop., A. E. Goodwin. 650 seats. Booked at Dublin. Continuous. Proscenium width, 25 ft. Prices, 1s. to 2s. 6d. Station, Limerick, C.I.E.

LYRIC (WE).—Prop., Amalgamated Cinemas (Ireland), Ltd., 9, Eden Quay, Dublin. 900 seats. Continuous. Prices, 1s. to 2s. 6d. Station, Limerick.

ROYAL CINEMA (WE). Cecil Street. Phone, Limerick 278.—Prop., Royal Cinema (Limerick), Ltd. 900 seats. Continuous. Prices, 1s. to 2s. 6d.

SAVOY THEATRE (WE). Bedford Row. Phone, Limerick 572.—Prop., Irish Cinemas, Ltd. 1,483 seats. Continuous. Prices, 1s. 3d. to 3s. Restaurant attached. Station, Limerick.

THOMOND (WE).—Prop., Thomond Cinema, Ltd. 500 seats.

TIVOLI (RCA). The Park.—Prop., Paul and May Bernard. 350 seats. Two shows nightly. Three changes weekly. Daily Mat.

LISMORE (Co. WATERFORD).

PALLADIUM (PARMEKO). Phone, Lismore 18.—Prop., D. Healy, M.D. 350 seats. Station, Lismore.

LISTOWEL (KERRY). Pop. 4,392.

ASTOR CINEMA (RCA).—Prop., P. Coffey. 500 seats.

PLAZA (WE). Phone, Tralee 95.—Prop. J. O'Sullivan. 600 seats. Nightly, two shows Sun. Occasional Variety. Station, Listowel, G.S.R.

LONGFORD (LONGFORD). Pop. 3,682.

ADELPHI CINEMA (RCA). Phone, Longford 57.—Prop., Midland Amusements Ltd., Bridge Street, Longford. 770 seats. Booked at H.O. One show nightly. Mat. Sun. Prices, 4d. to 1s. 8d. Four changes weekly. Café. Proscenium width, 45 ft. Station, Longford, C.I.E.

ODEON (WE). Bridge Street. Phone, Longford 57.—Prop., Midland Amusements, Ltd. Bridge Street, Longford. 609 seats. One show nightly. Mat. Sun. Prices, 1s. to 2s. 2d. Booked at H.O. Café. Proscenium width, 25 ft. Occasional Variety. Stage, 16 ft. deep. Two dressing-rooms. Station, Longford.

LOUGHREA (Co. GALWAY). Pop. 2,799.

TOWN HALL (RCA). Barrack Street. Phone, Loughrea 21.—Prop., Loughrea Town Hall, Ltd. 375 seats. Separate shows. Prices, 1s. to 2s. 2d. Four changes weekly. Booked at Hall. Screen, 15 ft. by 11 ft. Proscenium width, 16¼ ft. Stage, 17 ft. deep. Dance Hall attached. Station, Loughrea.

LUCAN (Co. DUBLIN).

PREMIER CINEMA (ELECTRA).—Prop., Lucan Cinemas, Ltd. 290 seats.

MACROOM (Co. CORK). Pop. 2,413.

CASTLE CINEMA (PHILIPS).—350 seats. Nightly. Four times weekly. Mat. Sun.

MALAHIDE (Co. DUBLIN). Pop. 1,200.

GRAND CINEMA (GB-KALEE). Phone, Malahide 236.—Prop., Mrs. K. Neilon-Wabb. 650 seats. One show daily. Mat., Sat. and Sun. Prices, 1s. 3d. to 2s. 3d. Café and Ballroom attached. Station, Malahide, G.N.R.

MALLOW (Co. CORK). Pop. 4,562.

CAPITOL.—Prop., Robinson and Ward. 300 seats. Nightly except Sat. Mat. Sun.

CENTRAL CINEMA (RCA). Main Street.—Prop., and Rev. Man., E. J. Donovan. 650 seats. Booked at Hall. Once nightly except. Sat. Mat. Sat. and Sun. Pictures and Variety. Telegrams. Donovan, Central Hall. Mallow.

MARYBOROUGH (LEIX). Pop. 3,382.

COLISEUM (WE).—Prop., Coliseum (Portleix), Ltd. 350 seats.

ELECTRIC CINEMA (AWH).—Prop., P. Delany. 400 seats. Booked at Hall. Once weekly, Sat. borough. One show nightly, Sat. excepted. Mat. Sun. Proscenium width, 19 ft. Station, Maryborough, C.I.E.

MIDLETON (Co. CORK). Pop. 3,182.

ORMONDE CINEMA (GB-KALEE). Phone, Midleton 17.—Prop., The Southern Star Cinema Co., Ltd. 700 seats. Booked at Dublin. Once nightly. Sun. Mat. Prices, 1s. 6d. and 2s. 3d. Four changes weekly. Proscenium width, 30 ft. CinemaScope. Station, Midleton, C.I.E.

MILFORD (Co. DONEGAL). Pop. 400.

LA SCALA (PARMEKO). Phone, Milford 30.—Prop., William McElwee. 285 seats. One show daily. Prices, 6d. to 1s. 6d. Four changes weekly. Booked at Dublin. Screen, 18 ft. by 12 ft. Station, Letterkenny. Films per Road Transport.

MILLSTREET (Co. CORK). Pop. 1,940.

THE CINEMA (WE).—Prop., D. McSweeney. 420 seats.

MITCHELSTOWN (Co. CORK). Pop. 2,011.

CENTRAL (KALEE).—Prop., Henry Delany. 600 seats.

STAR CINEMA (RCA). Church Road. Phone, Mitchelstown 4.—Prop., G. H. Sharp, Church Road. 400 seats. Booked at Hall. Once nightly. Mat. Sun. Four changes weekly. Prices, 4d. to 2s. Station, Knocklong.

MOATE (Co. WESTMEATH).

THE CINEMA (ERNEMANN).—Prop., Martin Fleming. 500 seats.

MOHILL (Co. LEITRIM). Pop. 755.

RITZ CINEMA (RCA). Globe Street.—Prop., F. J. Farrell, Clenooee, Longford. Phone, 50. 400 seats. One show nightly. Twice Sun. Booked at Longford. Proscenium width, 12 ft. Station, Mohill, G.S.R.

MONAGHAN (Co. MONAGHAN). Pop. 4,272.

MAGNET CINEMA (RCA).—Prop., Monaghan Cinemas, Ltd. 700 seats.

MOUNTMELLICK (LEIX). Pop. 2,502.

CYMS CINEMA (WE). Phone, Mountmellick 7.—Prop., P. A. Fennelly, 28, Emmet Street, 802 seats. One show nightly. Mat. Sun. Prices, 8d. to 2s. Five changes weekly. Booked at Dublin. Station, Mountmellick, C.I.E.

MOUNTRATH (Co. LAOIGHIS).

COLISEUM THEATRE.—Prop., John Egan.

MOVILLE (Co. DONEGAL).

COLISEUM (IMPERIAL).—Prop., John Egan. 375 seats.

MULLINGAR (Co. WESTMEATH). Pop. 5,293.

COLISEUM CINEMA (WE).—Prop., Counties Cinemas, Ltd. 314 seats. Booked at Dublin. Nightly, except Mon. Mat. Sun. Prices, 1s. and 1s. 8d. Station, Mullingar.

HIBERNIAN CINEMA (WE). Castle Street. Phone, Mullingar 2.—Prop., Counties Cinemas, Ltd. 770 seats. Prices, 1s. 3d. and 2s. 2d. Evenings continuous. Mat. Sat. Booked at Dublin. Proscenium width, 20 ft. Three dressing-rooms. Station, Mullingar, C.I.E.

NAAS (Co. KILDARE). Pop. 3,443.

COLISEUM (WE).—Prop., Egan, Kelly and Kelty. 700 seats.

NAVAN (MEATH). Pop. 3,649.

LYRIC CINEMA (WE).—Prop., Navan Picture Palace Co., Ltd., Brews Hill, Navan. Phone, 69. 857 seats. Once nightly. Mat. Sun. Booked at Dublin. Twice Sun. Variety. Proscenium width, 31 ft. Stage, 26 ft. Four dressing-rooms. Station, Navan, G.N.R., and C.I.E.

NAVAN PICTURE PALACE (ZEISS).—Prop., Navan Picture Palace Co., Ltd. Phone, Navan 69. 582 seats. Booked at Dublin. Once nightly. Mat. Sun. Proscenium width, 26 ft. Station, Navan, G.N.R. and C.I.E.

NENAGH (TIPPERARY). Pop. 4,517.

ORMONDE CINEMA (AWH).—Prop., Ormonde Cinema Co. 250 seats. Nightly five days a week. Mat., Sun. Prices, 4d. to 1s. 3d. Station, Nenagh, G.S.R.

RIALTO (WE).—Prop., Amalgamated Entertainment (Nenagh), Ltd. 900 seats.

NEWBRIDGE (Co. KILDARE). Pop. 2,400.

ODEON (WE). Main Street. Phone, Newbridge 47.—Prop., Newbridge Cinemas, Ltd. Phone, Dublin 92606 or Curragh 20. 720 seats. Once nightly. Four changes weekly. Prices, 1s. to 1s. 8d. Booked at Dublin. Proscenium width, 24 ft. Stage, 6 ft. Station, Newbridge.

PALACE (RCA). Henry Street. Phone, Newbridge 20.—Prop., Curragh Picture Co., Ltd., Picture House, Curragh Camp. 360 seats. One show daily. Prices, 1s. to 1s. 8d. Four changes weekly. Booked at Dublin. Station, Newbridge.

NEWCASTLE WEST (LIMERICK). Pop. 2,687.

DESMOND CINEMA (WE). Phone, Newcastle 25.—Prop., Patrick O'Carroll Nash, Demesne House, Newcastle West. 500 seats. Pictures and occasional Variety. Once nightly. Mats., Wed. and Sat. Booked at Newcastle West. Proscenium width, 22 ft. Stage, 10 ft. deep. Two dressing-rooms. Café and Dance Hall attached. Station, Newcastle West.

LATCHFORD'S CINEMA (MORRISON).—Mr. Latchford. 250 seats. Nightly, Tues. and Fri.

NEWMARKET (Co. CORK).

CASINO (WE).—Prop., Thomas G. Cooper. Phone, Killarney 25. 500 seats. One show Sun., Tues., Wed., Thurs. and Fri. Three changes weekly. Prices, 8d. to 1s. 8d. Booked at Dublin. Station, Banteer.

NEWMARKET-ON-FERGUS (Co. CLARE).

CENTRAL CINEMA (DEURY).—Prop., Richard Murray. 300 seats.

NEWPORT (Co. MAYO). Pop. 200.

NEW CINEMA (PHILIPS).—Prop., The Local Clergy. 250 seats. Shows Sun. and Mon. nights. Dance Hall attached. Rail to Westport and Road Transport.—(Closed).

NEW ROSS (WEXFORD). Pop. 6,000.

RITZ CINEMA (RCA).—Prop., Amalgamated Entertainments (New Ross), Ltd., 750 seats. Once nightly, Tues., Thurs. and Sat. Two shows, Mon., Wed. and Fri. Mat. Sun. Prices, 10d. to 2s. Mat., 8d. to 1s. 3d. Four changes weekly. Booked at Dublin. Station, New Ross.

OLDCASTLE (Co. MEATH). Pop. 927.

CASTLE CINEMA (WE). Oliver Plunkett Street. Phone, Oldcastle 10.—Prop., Oldcastle Cinemas, Ltd. 600 seats. One show daily. Two shows Sun. Four changes weekly. Prices, 1s. to 2s. Booked at Oldcastle. CinemaScope. Station, Oldcastle, G.N.R.

PASSAGE WEST (Co. CORK). Pop. 1,780.

C.Y.M.S. HALL (ZEISS-IKON).—Prop., Rev. J. C. O'Flynn. 357 seats. Two shows Sun., one show Wed. Two changes. Prices, 10d. to 1s. 6d. Booked at Dublin. Station, Cork, Dep.

POSTERS
Above left: The Searchers starring John Wayne
Above right: Ben Hur with Carlton Heston
Right: A Night at the Opera with the Marx
Brothers

Opposite above: Excel Cinema, Tipperary Town

*Opposite below: The Kinematograph Year Book,
1956,* RCA, which includes the Directory for
Eire, listing each town, its population and the
number of cinemas operating in the country

A display of merchandise for *Mary Poppins*, 1965

and I have been lucky enough in other instances. Yet it seems extraordinary that luck comes into it – that so few films fruitfully humour their source material, as *Great Expectations* does, as *Double Indemnity* and *Little Dorrit* do, as *The Age of Innocence* and *Ethan Frome* do. Telling the same story in photographic form is no mean feat. Rarely achieved, it is the cinema's most telling magic.

Ciaran Benson
The Sense of Wonder

I was perhaps four years old. My father led me by the hand through the big doors. He spoke to someone, led me up some steps, through doors that swung into darkness. We turned right and then left and immediately I saw something I had never imagined before. In front of me in huge bright light a man seemed to run towards me. There was a wall on his right as he ran, and as he did so he grew bigger and bigger until, reaching the end of the wall, he turned and ran in the opposite direction, getting smaller and smaller. This was my first glimpse of 'the pictures', in the Pavilion in Dun Laoghaire.

There were two remarkable aspects to this experience. One of these I never had repeated for me; the other has ever since been the basis of an enduring love affair. The first has to do with what in psychological studies of perception is called 'constancy'. When the distance between an object and an eye is halved, the size of the image on the retina is doubled, yet we do not see the object as being twice as big. The brain constantly adjusts to changes in the perceived world and works to dampen down such effects to keep the world relatively stable. In that first experience of the astonishing illusory world which is cinema, I believe I had a rare insight into what a perceptually inconstant world might look like. It never happened again, probably because my brain quickly got its sums right. But I have never lost the sense of wonder which was the second aspect of that experience. When the lights go out and the curtain opens, I feel myself falling again into yet another new world with its own look and lives and longings.

When I was six my father brought me to see something which I think was called *Smiley*; but I'm not sure, because of the more powerful impact of the Pathe News showing the tanks and people and ruins of the 1956

Hungarian Uprising. There was a sharp contrast between one type of 'picture' – the likes of *Smiley* – and another which had to do with the fragilities of 'the real world'. Again, a life-long interest and set of riddles about the real and the illusory began its gestation in the flickering darkness of the Pavilion.

For the rest of my childhood there was hardly a weekend that I did not spend in either the Pavilion or the Adelphi, or less frequently in the Astoria. It would be quite easy to use the alternative reality of the films I've seen over my lifetime to map a shadow-history of the changes in my 'real life' over the same period. The Astoria, the Pavilion and the Adelphi are long gone, but the Forum in Glasthule preserves a long tradition. The boundaries between light and dark, between what happens in front of and 'behind' the screen, between what is happening 'in' my head and 'before' my eyes, are mysterious and hard to find. There have been many times when I left a cinema with a sense of warm loss. Loss, because I felt that I'd been given privileged access to worlds and lives which were often more textured and real than the world I was returning to; but warm, because the magic of cinema includes the possibility of going back inside again.

Even now my memories of a certain period are in black and white, since so many images of that time, photographic and cinematic, were of necessity in black and white. For me, as for everyone who loves film, the nature of the world changed radically when I caught my first glimpse of cinema. A new pleasure was born as part of a new type of experience. Both have become fuller with the passing of time.

Deirdre Purcell
Moving Pictures

I was four or five years old and my mother and my aunt had promised to take me to see *The Robe* in the State Cinema in Phibsboro.

For days beforehand, they tried to explain to me about 'moving pictures'. There were pictures of people up on a big white sheet. And the pictures moved.

Like on a train? Did the pictures of the people move along the big white sheet like a train moving along the tracks?

No. The people moved. They moved like real people. But they were not real. They were bigger than real. But sort of flat. And they were in colour.

I couldn't get it. In a pre-television era, 'pictures' meant black-and-white snapshots or oil paintings; I found the concept of 'moving pictures' virtually impossible to imagine.

Each night before the Big Night, I tried to puzzle it out. Long lines of boxcars moved slowly across the big white sheet of my imagination, each car holding hordes of rigid cutout people, painted in shades of purple and magenta – the colours of my favourite crayons.

I got a new coat for the occasion. Princess line, six buttons, blue; cut down from someone else's cast-off. But it had a little velvet collar and I felt I was the bee's knees.

Going in, I got ice cream in a tub with a little wooden spoon. So far so good (although the ice cream was too hard and by the time I was able to get it out of the tub, it was dribbling all over my new coat). The foyer was redolent of feet, Jeyes Fluid, wet wool (from all the damp coats) and gusts of cheap perfume. Lily of the Valley. Ashes of Roses. 4711.

The cinema itself was huge. Frightening. And when the curtains swished, revealing the white sheet, when the sheet blazed so suddenly with all the colours of the rainbow and the startup music roared like a train across the seats, I was frightened half to death.

The people on the screen were huge. Their voices were huge. Their swords and clothes and hair were huge. Even the colours they wore were huge.

To this day, the moment in which the seamless robe wrapped itself around the neck of the vile Roman soldier at the foot of Jesus's cross, strangling him, rates as one of the most terrifying episodes of my life. I had nightmares about the scene for weeks, months afterwards.

And yet – and yet...

I went back to *Bambi* and *Old Yellow* and *Living Desert*, graduated to *The Song Of Bernadette*, *Gone With The Wind* and *Marcellino*, and ended up as a confirmed cinemaholic by the age of fourteen.

In some way I cannot properly express, *The Robe* grabbed me as tightly as it did that Roman soldier, opening up the infinite possibilities of the human imagination, the resource by which I now make my living.

Pat Murphy

Adults are more innocent than children. They take us to the pictures without realising that the most sentimental, innocuous films can be initiations into terror. I was taken to the pictures a lot when I was little, but for a long time, all I would talk about was the MGM lion. Nothing that followed could compare with the spectacle of that enormous fanged yawn.

The image that remains from Disney's *Sleeping Beauty* is of the Prince hacking his way through a forest of thorns to get to the Princess, and being confronted by the dragon. It stoops to finish him off. He plunges his sword upwards and almost staggers under the deluge of purple blood.

I was frightened of staircases. Just before going down one, I'd get a flash of myself lying at the bottom in a dark mess of blood and brains, and at the same time I'd have this bizarre urge to take a sudden leap and trust that I could fly. For years I thought this was just some Freudian thing, but then I remembered waking suddenly in the dark and seeing this woman somersault over and down the stairs. Her husband is standing at the top looking satisfied. I am in the Strand cinema on a Sunday afternoon; Cora Farrell, the girl next door, has carried me in while I was asleep.

As we get older, we lose that childhood awareness that films have lives of their own beyond the knowledge of the film-makers, meanings which leak in no matter how tight they seal the story.

I took my niece to see *Baron Munchhausen* and we had to leave because she was frightened by the disembodied head of the man in the moon. And this is a child who has seen *Jaws* about fifteen times.

I saw *The Song of Bernadette* three times – not from devotion, but because my grandfather took me to a matinée at the Rialto cinema and then fell asleep and I couldn't wake him up. What I remember most is people not believing her and then when she goes into a convent, the other nuns are mean and make her scrub floors. Even at the age of four, I could see that having visions was not the way to go.

Being brought into town to the Metropole was a special event. You looked forward to it for ages and played games about it afterwards. You got ice cream in a tub with a wooden spoon. There was an exciting smell to the dark. There were velvet seats and shining curtains and someone showed you to your seat with a beam of light. It was nothing like being sent out to the pictures on a Saturday afternoon, out of your mother's way, to a cinema where the toilets stank and kids ran screaming up and down the aisles. The worst thing was being made to take your little sister, who always wanted to go to the toilet ten minutes after the picture started. Once, I made her go on her own. She took ages and came back crying, but I was too absorbed in Hayley Mills and *In Search of Castaways* to take any notice. Years later she told me that two big girls had climbed in the window behind her and had taken her ticket and all her money.

Going to the cinema is still a childlike thing to do, despite how knowing audiences have become and how ingratiatingly film-makers collude with them. You sit in the dark, expectant, hoping something nice will happen. You arm yourself with supplies for the journey (popcorn and wine gums) and then you set off.

In fact, it's not just the experience of going to the cinema that's similar. I think that the very nature of watching movies mirrors the nature of childhood. Remember skies and seas so endless that your heart almost burst with the feeling that you were as limitless as the horizon. Yet insects under a stone could be as large. The blank intensity of sunlight. Faces as big as landscapes looming in and out of the darkness.

Only film can give us that fluid, displaced sense of scale, inspire us with the newnesss and richness of things, that feeling of reality being vividly itself and at the same time being like a skin or a veil which is about to fall away and reveal wonders.

Peter Sirr
Rituals

It is 11 am on a Friday morning and Father O'Connor is fiddling with the projector at the back of the assembly hall in which the school has been gathered. The ritual begins with technical difficulties, Father O'Connor threading the film and scratching his head. It has been decided to celebrate the end of term with a film – perhaps 'celebrate' is an exaggeration; to 'conclude' the term decorously with a suitable picture, a cowboy film, most likely. We're ranged in rows of hard chairs; there's a babble of not-quite-expectancy as the scratchy flickering stuff comes up on the screen. Then it begins: a man, a horse, a destination, a purpose. Stewart Granger shoots, is shot at. Cows run and make the discontented, put-upon noises of cows in cowboy films. Teachers gaze down the long rows to make sure we are paying attention.

How many times is it possible to see *The Guns of Navarone*? On they move towards the fortress: Gregory Peck, David Niven, Richard Harris and the others. I'm watching this in a makeshift cinema in, I think, Courtown, and then again in Fethard-on-Sea. The seats are hard. Even the locals seem to have seen the film before. Maybe it has been playing here since it was first released in 1961. I seem to remember Father O'Connor crouched over his projector, unleashing this on us too, to mark the end of yet another term, or perhaps to celebrate the victory of the senior team. This is the same hall where we are led in order to practise rugby chants, urging on the school with grim fervour. The favoured ones are cheer-leaders; the rest of us are cheered. Roughly exhorted, we raise our voices and chant. Male excitement fills the room. Anthony Quinn is Stavros, a brave Greek. The Germans are clever and ruthless.

There is this film about Poles and Cossacks. Yul Brynner I think is a Cossack, and Tony Curtis is in there somewhere too, doing his best not to falter under the hard but ultimately kindly gaze of Yul. The film contains the line 'The Poles are coming'. It contains other lines, but this is the only one I remember. My eyes are glued to the television which is perched just inside the door of my grandmother's kitchen. Visitors come in and thrust open the door. The television disappears. The visitors linger in the doorway, performing elaborate rituals of entrance. They may stay there all night. The door may never close again. What's happening? Through the frosted glass of the door comes the sound of hooves. Soon the battle will begin. Please let them come in and sit down, and please let no one talk to me. Then there will be the ceremony of departure, whose altar also is the doorway, the television sequestered like the Host in the tabernacle.

It is 1976 and I have entered the Stella in Rathmines with two friends in order to see *The Day of the Jackal*.

My friends are given their tickets. The ticket-seller looks at me and shakes her head. 'Under-fifteens accompanied by adults,' she says. I am seventeen. I have read the novel. My friends laugh. 'We'll tell you what happens. Now go home and don't stay up too late.'

Butch Cassidy or the Sundance Kid is very slowly undoing the buttons on her starchy white nightdress and then coiling a hand in around her waist. God, she is so beautiful!

The wily Cyril Cusack has sold him an ingenious gun which he conceals in the engine of his car. He buys a melon and drives to the woods. He gets out the gun and the melon and walks deep into the woods. He hangs the melon from a branch. He walks back, a long way back.

He aims, he fires. Splat, goes the melon.

I am sitting with my friends in the Classic in Terenure, waiting for *Chitty Chitty Bang Bang* to begin, when my own name appears on the screen in big letters, against a purple background. Happy Birthday, the screen says, and we are all amazed. How is this possible?

Why can I never enter a cinema alone? Because it is a theatre of love and I can only watch films publicly if I am in the presence of the beloved and the film is part of the conspiracy of desire. The film we are watching is also the film we are showing ourselves; it is *The night we saw...* It is already half memory. Otherwise it is not a film; otherwise I will weep inwardly when bidden to visit the Happy Ring House across the road, when urged to eat and drink before, during and after the film; otherwise it is *The desolation of solitary cinema-going...*

In the Dutch *bioscoop* the film is about to begin. But first there is the ritual of the steel box which is passed around. We are invited to contribute coins for charity. This happens in every cinema, before every picture. Happily, we give. It is organised and serious. The society functions.

When I first came to live here there was an ad campaign running on television. It began with a gloomy couple sitting down to an evening of television in a well-appointed sitting room. The couple was fretful; even the plants looked bored. Cut to the same couple sitting down to a meal in a brightly-lit restaurant, and later, entering a well-appointed cinema. They are smiling, they are happy, they are social. *It's pleasant to go out*, the slogan goes. The country listens, and is chastened.

Movies

Meanwhile our parents had made it, they were old hands
slouched in the wine-glow
of an endless dinner. Everything was authentic now
from the clothes worn to perfection
to the casual conviction of their voices
spilling out the open door. They were hitting their stride
and the house sat silent and absorbed,
watching, listening. Their lives were so well done
we are still struggling with our coats
in the threadbare plush,
still blinking at the lobby's air
of spent invitation,
pushing drugged limbs through a glass door
and disbelieving every step of the journey home.

Epilogue

As cinema celebrates its hundredth birthday, we hope that this book shows something of the pleasure and the pain of going to the pictures, for people ranging from the 'average' cinema-goer to – as we found in so many cases – the avid fan.

Their movie memories are often tinged with nostalgia – with mental maps of places which are long gone, ripped down to make way for shops or converted into skating rinks. The stories deal with the innocence of childhood, with that almost illicit feeling of being in a dark place with your best friends and complete strangers, from courting couples to torch-wielding figures of authority. These places in which we immersed ourselves, from the cinemas of small country towns to the picture-houses of the metropolis, were places which were familiar yet exotic. Surrounded by the smells of crisps and oranges, and that unmistakable whiff of a cinema's furnishings, we'd tuck ourselves up for a trip to the most faraway of worlds. This was where we began to learn ways of laughing and crying, of heckling and imitating, in (that catchphrase of the 1990s) an 'interactive multimedia experience'.

There remains a lovely paradox about the cinema. It's a public place but also a very private space. In this sense, it's like the memories recorded here: in the weft and warp of the individual echoes and personal responses is a mapping of a social and collective memory. Perhaps as we grow older – and as the cinema itself becomes older – we begin to forget the kind of abandon, the power of the image, the desire in the dark, that re-emerge in these memories; and perhaps we need occasional reminders of them.

We also need reminding that the cinema is a sort of triangle between (a) everybody involved in making a film, from the director and the top stars to the key grips and best boys; (b) the films themselves; and (c) the people who actually go to see them. In everyday life, plenty is written about the first two (the producers and their products), but the third essential element – the audience – often slips totally out of the picture (no pun intended).

A common theme among the preceding essays is that many of the writers grew up in a time when cinema-going was a special event, when films hardly had a life outside the local cinema or the draughty school hall. Images were fleeting and ephemeral – and perhaps were treasured all the more for being so – and were shown in public spaces rather than ordinary homes. Domestic video recorders hadn't yet become standard in every household, and television had not reached the 57-varieties around-the-clock flow we have today, with specialist channels devoted to the latest movies or to cinema classics and mainstream terrestrial stations showing hours and hours of filmed drama each week.

Here, in these echoes, we glimpse the cinema's unique power to transport us, to mould and mirror, to shape and seduce, to divert and entertain – for one night only and for the rest of our lives...

Stephanie McBride

NOTES ON CONTRIBUTORS

Mary Banotti represents Dublin as an MEP.

Ray Bates is the Director of the National Lottery.

Patrick Bergin was born in Dublin and now lives and works as an actor in Los Angeles.

Ciaran Benson was born in Dublin. He is Professor of Psychology at University College, Dublin and is Chairman of the Arts Council/An Comhairle Ealaíon.

Agnes Bernelle was born in Berlin but has worked as a chanteuse in Dublin, where she has lived since the 1940s.

Maeve Binchy was born in Dublin and is an international best-selling author. She also writes a weekly column for the *Irish Times*.

Dermot Bolger is a writer and publisher living in Dublin.

Maxine Brady was formerly president of the Union of Students in Ireland and now works as a freelance journalist.

Gabriel Byrne grew up in Dublin and is now one of Ireland's best-known screen actors.

Gay Byrne is Ireland's best-known broadcaster and presenter of the longest-running television chat show in the world, *The Late Late Show*.

Michael Colgan is the director of the Gate Theatre, Dublin.

Evelyn Conlon is a writer from Co. Monaghan, now based in Dublin.

Shane Connaughton is a writer from Co. Cavan.

June Considine grew up in Finglas, Dublin. She writes novels for children and young adults, and edits *Futura* Magazine.

Mary Cummins is a staff journalist with the *Irish Times*.

Cyril Cusack was one of Ireland's best-known and most celebrated actors.

Father Brian D'Arcy grew up in County Fermanagh and is arguably Ireland's best-known cleric. He contributes a weekly column to the *Sunday World*.

Luke Dodd is former director of the Famine Museum, Strokestown House, and is currently Head of Archives at the Film Institute of Ireland.

Lelia Doolan is currently Chair of Bord Scannan na hÉireann/Irish Film Board. She has worked in theatre, television and film and now lives in Galway.

Joe Duffy was born in Dublin and is a journalist and broadcaster.

Myles Dungan co-founded the Dublin Film Festival and works as a broadcaster.

Michael Dwyer co-founded the Dublin Film Festival in 1986 and is film correspondent for the *Irish Times*.

John Feehan grew up in Laois and works as an environmentalist.

Frank Feely is a Dubliner and former City Manager.

Garret Fitzgerald is an economist, former Taoiseach and former leader of Fine Gael.

Sandy Fitzgerald was born in Dublin and is director of the City Arts Centre.

Brenda Gannon lives in Dublin and is the administrator with the Federation of Irish Film Societies.

Michael Garvey is a senior producer in RTÉ television.

Luke Gibbons grew up in Co. Roscommon. He lectures in Film and Cultural Studies at Dublin City Unversity.

Alan Gilsenan has been a documentary film-maker for over a decade. He is currently in pre-production on his first screen fiction.

Mary Harney is the Leader of the Progressive Democrats and is a member of Dáil Éireann.

Seamas Hosey grew up in Co. Laois. He is a producer and broadcaster with RTÉ radio.

Bill Hughes was born in Kildare and is an independent television producer.

Marina Hughes grew up in Kilmactranny in Co. Sligo. She now lives in Dublin and works as a film producer.

John Kavanagh is a stage and screen actor, living in Dublin.

Richard Kearney was born in Cork. He is Professor of Philosophy at University College, Dublin and has recently published his first novel.

Albert Kelly is Chairman of the Independent Cinema Owners Association and has owned and run the Classic cinema in Harold's Cross, Dublin, since 1976.

Brendan Kennelly, Professor of English Literature at Trinity College, Dublin, is also a poet, dramatist and novelist.

Benedict Kiely was born in Co. Tyrone and is a writer, journalist and broadcaster.

Jimmy Lacey is a freelance journalist, born, living and working in Wexford.

Tim Lehane grew up in Co. Cork and is a senior producer with RTE radio.

Hugh Leonard writes plays, films and television scripts and lives in Dalkey.

Karl MacDermott is a comedian who grew up in Galway and now lives in Dublin.

Liz MacManus is the Democratic Left TD for Wicklow.

John MacMahon grew up in Co. Kerry. He works as a commissioning editor for educational programmes with RTÉ.

Laura Magahy is the managing director of Temple Bar Properties and a member of the Arts Council.

Sam McAughtry grew up in Belfast. He is a writer and raconteur and a member of the Senate.

Hugh McCabe was born in Kilkenny. He emigrated to America but now lives in Dublin, where he lectures in Electronic Engineering at Dublin City University.

Pat McCabe is a novelist and playwright from Clones, Co. Monaghan. His novel *The Butcher Boy* is being adapted for film.

Nell McCafferty is a writer and journalist who was born in Derry and now lives in Dublin.

Frank McGuinness was born in Buncrana, Co. Donegal. He is a playwright and poet and lectures in English in St Patrick's College, Maynooth.

John MacKenna was born in Castleldermot, Co. Kildare. He is a writer and commissioning editor for RTÉ radio.

Clare McKeon is a broadcaster based in Dublin.

Louis Marcus was born in Cork. He is a film director and has recently completed a series on the Irish Famine for television.

Pat Murphy is a film director living in Dublin. She is currently working on a film about Nora Barnacle.

Bryan Murray, a stage and screen actor, was born in Dublin. He is now based in Los Angeles.

Doireann Ní Bhriain is a member of the Board of the Dublin Film Festival and was the commissioner for the *Imaginaire Irlandais* exhibition in France in 1996.

David Norris is a Joycean scholar and a member of the Senate, representing Trinity College, Dublin.

Harvey O'Brien grew up in Kilrush, Co. Clare. He now lives and works in Dublin as a freelance writer and lecturer.

Joe O'Connor was born in Dublin in 1963. He is a novelist and scriptwriter and a columnist with the *Sunday Tribune*.

Nuala O'Faolain is a writer and broadcaster and a columnist with the *Irish Times*.

Pat O'Mahoney grew up in Kildare. He is a broadcaster with RTÉ.

Mary O'Rourke represents Longford-Westmeath in Dáil Éireann.

Thaddeus O'Sullivan is a film director.

Maureen Potter is one of Ireland's best-known and loved performers – synonymous with pantomime at the Gaiety.

Deirdre Purcell is a best-selling author who was born and lives in Dublin.

Bob Quinn is an independent film-maker living and working in Connemara.

Feargal Quinn is a Dublin-based senator.

John Quinn grew up in Ballivor, Co. Westmeath. He now lives in Dublin, working as a broadcaster in RTÉ radio.

Kathleen Quinn was born in Monaghan and came to Dublin in 1932. Now retired, she lives in England, where she worked as a nurse during World War II.

Ruth Riddick grew up in Dublin and works in Public Relations. She is a trustee of the Projects Arts Centre.

Billy Roche is an award-winning playwright from Wexford. His first film, *Trojan Eddie*, has recently been completed.

Kevin Rockett was born in Co. Kilkenny and is a film historian now living in Dublin. He has recently published *The Irish Filmography*.

Peter Sirr is a poet and the director of the Irish Writers' Centre.

Sheamus Smith is the Film Censor.

Gerry Stembridge was born in Limerick and is a writer, playwright and film director.

Eamonn Sweeney lives and works in Dublin as a researcher for RTÉ Radio. His first novel, *Waiting for the Healer*, will be published by Picador in 1997.

Chalmers (Terry) Trench lives in Drogheda and established the Drogheda Branch of the Irish Film Society in 1945.

William Trevor was born in Ireland and is an internationally acclaimed writer. He is now living in England.

Eibhear Walshe grew up in Waterford. He lectures in English at University College, Cork.

Liam Wylie was born in Dublin. He works in the archive section of the Film Institute of Ireland and is currently working on a documentary film.

LEADING HOLLYWOOD
Áine O'Connor

'Ireland has more natural actors than anywhere I've ever been...
I think it's something you learn for survival.' Aidan Quinn

For the first time in the history of Hollywood, there are six romantic leading actors from a country other than the US – and it's Ireland.

Gabriel Byrne, Liam Neeson, Patrick Bergin, Stephen Rea, Aidan Quinn, Pierce Brosnan: They've made it in Hollywood as leading international screen stars whose names alone can make a movie.

Now, in frank and intimate interviews with film-maker and actress Aine O'Connor, Ireland's best-loved movie stars speak straight from the heart. They give the inside story on the 'Dream Machine' that is Hollywood; they share their childhood memories and their hopes for the future; they talk about trying to withstand the pressures that go with stardom, about their thoughts on acting, love and success, about how their Irish identity has shaped them and remained part of them - and about how they have managed to survive and succeed in one of the toughest industries in the world.

Illustrated with photographs of the actors' childhoods, their early days as rising stars, their best-known movies, their Hollywood lives and more.

Book of forthcoming major TV series and video
ISBN 0 86327 556 7

PICTURES IN MY HEAD
Gabriel Byrne

A WOLFHOUND BESTSELLER

'An evocative and entertaining volume.'
Irish Times

'Whether it's getting drunk in Venice with Richard Burton, remembering the immigrant friends he met on the way or witnessing the birth of his son, Jack Daniel, Byrne magically captures the moment.'
Sunday Independent

From his first ever visit to the cinema to his work on film sets *Pictures in My Head* tracks Gabriel Byrne the actor and the man with a disarming frankness and self-effacing humour.

ISBN 0 86327 462 5

Available from Wolfhound Press
68 Mountjoy Square
Dublin 1
Tel: (01) 8740354